THE FLOWER ARRANGER'S GARDEN

THE FLOWER ARRANGER'S GARDEN

ROSEMARY VEREY

PHOTOGRAPHY BY
LINDA BURGESS

LITTLE, BROWN AND COMPANY
BOSTON · TORONTO · LONDON

Library of Congress Catalog Card Number: 88-82540

First published in 1989 in the United Kingdom by
Conran Octopus Limited

10 9 8 7 6 5 4 3 2 1

Bt 29.95/16.11- 5/90

The publishers would like to thank the following for their
generous assistance: Fiona Barnett; Rosemary Butler; Audrey
Clark and Giles Clark; Eve's Lace, Antiquarius, 135 King's Road,
London SW3; The Gallery of Antique Costume and Textiles, 2 Church
Street, London NW8; Julia Hodgkin and Ernestine Dyer, The Flower
Shop, The Heal's Building, 196 Tottenham Court Road, London W1;
Mrs Monro, 11 Montpelier Street, London SW7; Pillows of London,
48 Church Street, London NW8; Richard Edwards Ceramics,
The Endell Street Place, Endell Street, London WC2; Ann Lingard,
Rope Walk Antiques, Rye, Sussex; Tobias and the Angel, 68 White Hart
Lane, Barnes, London SW13; Mary Verey; Timothy Walker.

Printed and bound in Italy
Amilcare Pizzi S.p.a.

CONTENTS

INTRODUCTION

This is a book for gardeners who are also flower arrangers, for those people who find it a joy to go out into the garden with basket and secateurs and wander round it contemplating what to cut and how to arrange the pickings indoors. I hope that it will make it possible to achieve the impossible – to have plenty of flowers and leaves for cutting and yet also to have full and colourful borders. This requires quite a lot of thought, planning, and skill both in growing and in careful cutting. It also requires imagination.

Skill includes making sure the flowers that are in bloom simultaneously have matching, blending or complementary colours. The same is true for foliage: the background of your vases is as important as the background of your borders, so you must grow enough evergreen and deciduous shrubs to be able to pick a fair number of leaves and branches, buying or begging others to supplement your own.

Many years ago, in August 1947 to be precise, a weekend guest asked me if she might do a great big arrangement for the centre of my drawing room. When I apologized for the lack of flowers in the garden, she took no notice and very soon had created a superb mixture of differently textured leaves with the minimum of flowers. This was an eye-opener to me and I remember her with gratitude to this day. She taught me a lesson.

I find it absolutely invaluable, as part of the constant process of learning about gardening, to have a notebook, preferably with a hard cover, in which to make memos of the flower combinations I have enjoyed and to build up the list of plants I would like to grow in my garden and see in my house. You think you will remember them, but I can guarantee that you won't. When you are making your lists, add a few notes about the height, colour, preferred growing conditions and – most important – the time of flowering. Note down the spot in your garden you have in mind; by the time you get round to buying the plant, your colour scheme and planning ideas may have changed, but you will be reminded of why you liked it in the first place.

Another skill which enthusiasm and experience will bring is the ability to be canny about spaces – to think of and make use of all the odd garden corners other than borders where you can tuck extra flowers, to use some plants as coat-hangers for climbers to drape themselves over, and to become accustomed to planting in layers. The flower arranger in you will be grateful for the extra picking material this contriving will provide throughout the year.

I believe that the art of flower arranging is changing. We are becoming less pleased with the very formal, rather stiff arrangements which have been popular and fashionable since the last war. I have much admiration for those lovely bouquets full of expensive florist's flowers, often flown in from abroad, but to me a vase full of wild flowers, put in almost as casually as they might be growing in a meadow, is just as beautiful.

If you think about this, you will probably find on reflection that your preference is decidedly for the one kind of flower or the other. Hybrid Teas or Damasks? Chrysanthemums or peonies? Hydrangeas or hellebores? To achieve a well-balanced but exuberant garden you should try to re-educate your natural inclinations, including a wider range of plants so that your borders have a rhythm and variety in shapes, textures and colours to last all the year. Space in this book has allowed only sixty-four plants to be discussed in detail, but space in your garden will, I hope, be more generous to you.

In trying to increase the range of flowers and foliage you wish to grow, remember that it is a good idea to differentiate between the front garden and the back. Your front garden should look neat and colourful at all times. It is the place for tidy, shapely shrubs – skimmias and hebes, eleagnus, santolina and *Viburnum tinus* – and for neat-flowered perennials – iris, hostas, hellebores, even *Sedum* 'Autumn Joy'. It will provide the opportunity for plenty of tulips and daffodils and annuals planted between the shrubs. The annuals you can grow yourself or buy from the garden centre; a tray costing £3 will become £30-worth of cut flowers, while a hundred tulip bulbs cost ten times less than their equivalent in florist's bunches.

Your back garden will be different in character – a place to read, relax and entertain. It should provide somewhere to sit in sun and shade, be surrounded by a sequence of scents and have a strong design filled with a careless rapture of planting. In the planning chapter I hope you will find a border of a shape, size and aspect to suit your particular plot and which you may find useful as an inspiration for your own ideas.

A final word: always plant the best. It will not take up any more space than the second best, and although it may mean seeking out an unusual form, when you have added it to all the other special varieties you have found, your garden and your vases will reflect your character and have a style of which you can be proud.

PLANNING THE GARDEN

The exciting thing about planning any garden is the way it is forever changing. As you watch it develop from January through to December, you can decide and record how to make improvements for the next year as each month comes and goes. Imagination is important, too: seeing a patch of spring flowers when you plant your bulbs in the autumn, visualizing what the garden will look like in a few years' time when newly planted trees and shrubs have put on growth and filled out.

If you are a keen flower arranger, planning and planting has an extra dimension: you will want to have as many flowers and as much foliage as possible to pick and bring indoors, while requiring the garden to stay full of interest, not shorn of its treasures.

The flowers and foliage must also be in harmony – it is difficult to produce a really unhappy combination in the garden, but care is needed when planting flowers for bringing indoors.

◆

RICH BLOCKS OF COLOUR

The golds, crimsons and purples of late summer – crocosmia, heleniums, salvia, golden rod, and sedum about to turn red – massed in a broad border, will sustain interest in the garden and provide picking material for the house through into autumn.

FIRST THOUGHTS BEFORE PLANNING OR PLANTING

Before settling down to choosing trees and planning your beds, think about your needs and the pattern of your life. You will make fewer initial mistakes and save yourself time and money. Which months do you have most time to devote to flower arranging, and when do you usually go on holiday? During the school holidays you may find you are too busy to pick flowers. There will be some occasions when you regularly want to have the house filled with flowers. Important birthdays or anniversaries, weddings or weekend parties will require large arrangements, and if you are a bridge player or like to entertain friends to dinner you will want to make at least a centrepiece for the dining-room table or a pretty arrangement in the hall. House guests will appreciate a posy on their dressing table or on an upstairs window sill.

What sort of flower arrangements most appeal to you? If you enjoy making big, bold, formal groups, you will need branches cut from fast-growing shrubs to make a background in a vase, tall perennials and smaller flowers – annuals perhaps – with substantial heads to mass in the front. If, like one of my gardening friends, you love small delicate things and want to create jewel-like posies where every detail counts and demands attention, you will grow violets, pansies and primroses instead of sunflowers, delphiniums and dahlias. If you like country bunches, seemingly poked into a vase or basket at random but magically creating a lovely effect of tossing colour, your task will be easier – you can gather here and there in the garden as the fancy takes you, and supplement your pickings from the fields and hedgerows. Containers are important, too: if you have a cherished vase of deep blue or glowing red glass, you will want to grow flowers to complement its beauty.

The next stage is to look at your house and its decoration. Consider at which vantage points in the house your arrangements will look best, catch the light and create an impact. Sometimes a single bloom can say as much as a whole vaseful. A solitary white flower of the 'Cherokee Rose', *Rosa laevigata*, backed by dark shining leaves on a small table in the centre of a room in a house in Melbourne entranced each arriving guest. With its profusion of stamens it looked almost like a camellia. If you are out at work all day and want your rooms to look their best in the evening, choose colours and shapes which come into their own by electric or candlelight. It is an important truth that while plants in the garden rarely clash with each other – pinks, oranges, reds and purples, or shades or blue, yellow or green, living together in perfect harmony – flower tones when brought indoors must agree with walls and curtains. This may be straightforward – most of us tend to use colours which co-ordinate – but certain flowers, roses, for instance, have become so finely colour-graded that you can be certain of finding the exact shade to match your drawing-room curtains or kitchen wallpaper. Take the trouble to find and grow it for special occasions.

FRAGRANCE THROUGH THE YEAR

When choosing your plants, do not forget scent in the midst of all the considerations of colour, flowering time and aspect. Remember all the fragrant flowers you can have throughout the year and plant some for every season.

Winter has a wide range of fragrant shrubs: wintersweet and winter honeysuckle, some of the viburnums and sarcoccoca. The sweetest-scented small bulb is *Iris unguicularis*, which will flower in winter and early spring. If you have a sunny window sill, grow one or two of the fragrant-leaved pelargoniums, which can then stand outside in summer. My favourite is *Pelargonium* 'Mabel Grey'. For spring you might include all the scented narcissi, lily of the valley, *Iris reticulata*, osmanthus, daphne, mahonia, and yet more viburnums. There are too many to name for the summer border, but do not forget the roses. Autumn seems less well provided with scents, but you could use *Spartium junceum*, myrtle and two autumn-flowering honeysuckles, *Lonicera japonica* 'Halliana' and *L. periclymenum* 'Serotina'.

There are a few plants which are especially scented in the evening and at night. Often you only realize this when walking round the garden as night falls. For a sheltered wall try growing cestrum – the best for evening fragrance are *Cestrum aurantiacum*, *C. nocturnum* and *C. parqui*. The scent of tobacco plants – *Nicotiana affinis* and *N. sylvestris* – increases as the light fades and as they are brought into the warmth of the sitting room.

FLEETING BLOSSOM *The glorious display of spring blossom is brief and vulnerable; storms can too quickly throw down a carpet of pink or white. But branches of blossom should be included in at least one spring vase, and the armful waiting here of white, blue and clear green – blossom, lilac, bluebells, forget-me-nots, muscari, tulips and alchemilla – will make a ravishing arrangement for a spring party or a wedding.*

SUITING THE SITUATION *Whether you are planting a shady corner of a terrace (top), a sunny border (above), or a bed with a mixture of sun and shade (right), it is important to match the needs of the flowers and shrubs you choose with the realities of the site. Planted in hostile conditions the plants will not thrive.*

MARRYING PLANTS AND GARDEN

When you have carefully considered the flowers and foliage you most want to use in your arrangements, draw up a list, then compare the needs of your plants with the realities of your garden and all its idiosyncrasies. Put the flowers into categories – shade, sun, damp – which will help you decide the most appropriate sites for your borders. If you are creating new borders, you may be able to make them face the way that most suits your favourite plants; if the aspect of your borders is already fixed, you will have to select flowers to suit the site. You may need a sunny bed and a shady one. Remember the difference between the north side of an island bed and the south side. Decide if you would prefer one large border or two or three smaller ones. I think it is important to be able to enjoy flower borders from the window, also to put them near where you sit outside and you walk most often. Do make the best of any wall space or fence you have, and try to make the area round your front door look inviting.

Try to grow as much as you can yourself, but think about, and perhaps omit from your garden, those flowers which are long-lasting in water and which may be bought economically from the florist such as alstroemerias, spray carnations and chrysanthemums in season. Think beyond the qualities you usually associate with certain plants – their flowers, for instance, or their fruits – and make them multi-purpose, providing flowers, leaves and berries in due season, shading the ground for tender plants or acting as host for climbers. Remember too, that some plants used out of context can come as a delightful surprise – parsley leaves make a light and beautiful background for violas and pansies.

With all these thoughts crowding your mind, it is a good idea to make a plan, however rough, of the garden. Design the shape of the beds on paper first, then go out and, with a few bamboo sticks and some string, outline them on the ground. On paper again, draw in your chosen plants, making allowance for their final size, and only when you are satisfied go out and put the plants themselves in position or fix sticks and labels to mark the plants you have yet to buy. Then walk round and look at your placings from all angles – near to, from the house and further away.

It is worth taking this initial trouble, especially in a small garden, and if you have planned carefully, I guarantee that you will be amazed by how many things you will be able to pick without spoiling the effect you have created. With a slightly larger garden you may be able to fit in several borders, each facing a different direction, which will give you more choice, less agonizing over competing favourites.

Above all, if you are a gardener, disabuse yourself of the idea that it is a sin to rob the garden to adorn the house. With thought and enthusiastic planting you can do both.

A FRONT GARDEN

This bed for a front garden, 8 yards (metres) wide and 12 yards (metres) at its longest point, is planned mostly for summer going on through autumn, but has enough evergreens and spring flowers to provide material for winter and spring arrangements as well. It is designed for a garden where the gate is to one side of the front boundary fence. The plan can be reversed for a garden where the gate lies on the opposite side, and for a house with a wide double frontage, with a path running up the centre, the border could be repeated in mirror image.

Assuming that there is a fence or hedge along the road and also one dividing neighbour from neighbour, I have planted trees and shrubs along these two sides – five evergreens for year-round appeal, five for spring and summer blossom, and a few chiefly for their autumn berries. The two small deciduous trees give height to the bed: *Pyrus calleryana* 'Chanticleer' which grows in a pyramid shape, with white blossom and autumn colour, and *Malus* 'Red Sentinel' whose glossy scarlet fruits hang on right through the winter. The evergreen shrubs – eleagnus and holly, *Viburnum tinus* and garrya – provide winter substance as well as berries and flowers. I have not put a tree in the corner believing that an evergreen shrub would look better there. Hebe and rosemary, both good for picking, are placed to emphasize the corners of the border. The deciduous shrubs have been chosen for their spread of flowers – ribes and forsythia in spring, philadelphus and kolkwitzia in summer, followed by the buddleia.

The edging is planned to include both leaf form and flowers: pulmonaria, *Stachys lanata*, purple sage, narcissi, *Nigella damascena*, hostas, *Nepeta mussinii* and *Sedum* 'Autumn Joy'. Behind are groups of herbaceous plants, with pink tulips and forget-me-nots followed by white dahlias, and white narcissi followed by nigella.

SPRING

16

PLANTING KEY

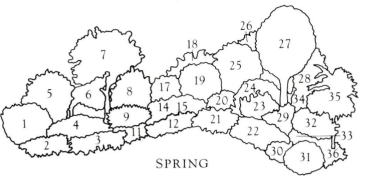

SPRING

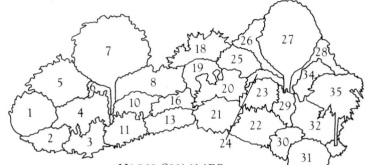

HIGH SUMMER

1 Rosemary
2 Pulmonaria
3 *Stachys lanata*
4 Aquilegia
5 *Kolkwitzia amabilis*
6 *Clematis montana*
7 *Malus* 'Red Sentinel'
8 *Garrya elliptica*
9 Narcissi (white)
10 *Nigella damascena*
11 Purple sage
12 *Primula* 'Barnhaven'
13 *Viola cornuta* 'Belmont Blue'
14 Tulips (pink)
15 Forget-me-nots
16 Dahlias (white)
17 *Viburnum tinus* 'Eve Price'
18 *Buddleia fallowiana* 'Lochinch'
19 *Ribes sanguineum* 'Brocklebankii'
20 Agapanthus
21 Hostas
22 *Nepata mussinii*
23 *Chrysanthemum maximum*
24 *Artemisia* 'Powis Castle'
25 Forsythia
26 *Elaeagnus × ebbingei*
27 *Pyrus calleryana* 'Chanticleer'
28 *Philadelphus* 'Belle Etoile'
29 *Acanthus mollis*
30 *Sedum* 'Autumn Joy'
31 *Hebe rakaiensis*
32 *Cornus alba* 'Elegantissima'
33 Muscari
34 Ilex (green)
35 *Cotoneaster × hybridus pendulus*
36 *Convallaria majalis*

HIGH SUMMER

PLENTY FOR CUTTING
WITHOUT SACRIFICING BORDERS

Choosing plants to suit one another and your garden, and massing them to advantage in length, depth and height, are two fundamentals for the gardener who is also a flower arranger. If you are using beds and borders to grow flowers for arrangements as well as to create a beautiful garden, you cannot afford to be self-indulgent and devote a large space to a plant which is ravishingly, but fleetingly, beautiful in flower, and which does not have leaves you can use indoors – *Paeonia mlokosewitschii*, for example. You will have to ration yourself to just a few of certain favourite plants – one or two hostas or hellebores will provide a good supply for picking, even though you might like to have a whole bedful. You must use every inch of ground, thinking in terms of planting in layers. If you can use a shrub which is attractive in itself as a prop for a climber as well, so much the better.

There are several combinations to consider when planning: plants which flower at the same time, complementing each other both in the garden and indoors, and the good companions, which enjoy being planted close to one another but which bloom at different seasons – as the flowers of one are spent, those of the other take over. There are the flowers of one plant which look good with the leaves of another, and there are different leaves which combine well.

PLANTING IN LAYERS

Vertical planting, or planting in layers, is almost a mathematical exercise. With care you can have the air space in any one small patch of ground occupied by up to half a dozen different plants at once. For example, at ground level might be spring-flowering forget-me-nots (later to be pulled up)

18

growing between hardy summer-flowering geraniums – *Geranium endressii* 'Wargrave Pink' or *G*. 'Johnson's Blue' – which will later spread out to cover this piece of ground. Piercing through them could be various early or late tulips, with a canopy of arching *Spiraea × arguta* flowering in late spring. Continuing upwards, and all in the same vertical picture, you might plant an upright-growing, spring-flowering tree with pretty summer leaves, *Prunus* 'Amanogawa' or *P. × 'hillieri'*, or perhaps *Gleditsia triacanthos* 'Sunburst', whose striking foliage is golden when young and turns yellow in autumn.

The massing of plants is all-important in an arranger's garden. Put in more than you think you need, but remember when you plant like this to feed with a nitrogen fertilizer for a quick boost to the foliage, or with a slow-release bonemeal for general well-being. Plants which are massed close together will need more frequent dividing in autumn or spring. In a small garden do not make each clump of the same plant too big. You may find you can tuck two or three extra plants of the varieties you use most in your arrangements in an out-of-the-way corner kept especially for picking – behind the garage or between your vegetables – so that you need only raid a few from the border. I am thinking of agapanthus, alstroemerias, astrantias, and scabious.

Do not rule out the idea of a picking bed. It may be quite small, but you will be able to cut every flower from it without spoiling the look of your borders. If you have a vegetable patch, you can make it look more attractive by surrounding it with a narrow picking border of colourful annuals and perennials. Real cottage gardens, in fact, often had strips of cutting flowers between the ranks of carrots and cabbages. You could perhaps update this notion by creating lines of colour in the different shades of the rainbow, the bands changing colour season by season.

FLOWERS THAT THRIVE ON CUTTING

Cut-and-come-again flowers are an absolute boon to the flower arranger. *Chrysanthemum maximum* and the yellow daisy, *Anthemis tinctoria*, are the first to spring to mind: both send up new flowering shoots soon after picking. The perennial *Delphinium elatum* and the annual *D. ajacis* (larkspur) have subsidiary flowering shoots up their tall stems, and if you pick the leader it gives these laterals a chance to develop. You will sacrifice some height in the border by doing so, but not colour. Polyanthus and primulas have a supply of potential flowering stems to come through, so you can afford to cull a selected few of the earliest. Pick them as the first of the multi-flowers on the stem are opening and more will come out in water after a day or two. The early-flowering pulmonarias have the same useful characteristic, and violas and pansies love being picked.

You will become adept at finding the blooms which are hiding behind leaves or behind one another, like shy people at a party. Pick them and give them pride of place in an arrangement. You can do the same with shrubs, but when the back of the shrub is less vigorous than the front it is advisable to cut the front branches hard back, almost to the main stem, to let more light in behind.

GENEROUSLY FILLED BORDERS *Massing plants and putting in more than you think you will need will ensure that a border will not be impoverished after picking for arrangements (left). But the ground must be well fed if it is to support planting in this quantity.*

MAKING USE OF THE AIR SPACE *A vertical picture is created (below) by planting* Stachys lanata *around the base of the pale pink rose 'Grüss an Aachen'. Above it is a purple* Cotinus coggygria *with the climbing rose 'Parade' as the final layer.*

COLOURING IN THE GAPS *Ground cover plants inserted at the base of leggy plants such as campanula (top) or asters (above) make the maximum use of space and improve the appearance of the border. They are also an often-forgotten source of material for small posies or trailing fronds to soften the base of an arrangement.*

GROUND COVER PLANTS

Difficult places and more or less hidden territory can be occupied by ground cover plants. Under trees where it may be very dry try a carpet of evergreen *Pachysandra terminalis.* A display of glistening white, cress-like flowers tinged with purple appears in early spring. Other plants suitable for carpeting under trees are bergenias and the only lime-tolerant lithospermum, *L. caeruleum.* Both *Vinca major* and *V. minor,* also accommodating plants which thrive in poor and shady

soil, will provide plenty of starry flowers – blue, mauve and white – for posies, and glossy strands of foliage to soften the lower edges of larger arrangements.

The virtue of these ground cover plants, and others such as ivies, dicentra, epimedium, tolmeia, lamium and *Alchemilla mollis,* is that you can pick their leaves liberally without making inroads and gaps in the picture.

Ferns have much the same function as ground cover plants – they are tough and long-lived, and may be tucked into odd corners which do not necessarily form part of the border. I feel that their fronds look more at home in the company of leaves and feathery herbs than they do as a background to flowers in the usual florist's arrangements.

USING EVERY SCRAP OF SPACE

You will find that the habit of growth of many plants gives you the opportunity of fitting in others close around or under them. First there are the herbaceous plants which become leggy and untidy with dying leaves at their base – delphiniums and phlox, for instance. Put lower-growing plants immediately in front of them, such as monarda, *Nepeta* 'Six Hills Giant', *Euphorbia palustris* or *E. characias* subsp. *wulfenii.* Then there are the evergreen shrubs – skimmia, mahonia, osmanthus and rosemary – whose lower branches are bare of foliage, particularly as the plant ages. Select for the foreground a plant whose leaves complement the evergreen in colour and texture. *Tellima grandiflora* 'Purpurea' could be planted in front of mahonia or osmanthus. Chives or *Ophiopogon planiscapus* 'Nigrescens', with dark purple strap-shaped leaves, would look well grouped round rosemary, and Bowles' golden grass or *Festuca glauca* could encircle a skimmia. Finally there are all the deciduous shrubs like philadelphus, forsythia, syringa, jasmine and kolkwitzia, whose bare winter stems may be surrounded with flowering plants and bulbs before their own leaves appear. My choice is hellebores, *Iris reticulata* chionodoxas, scillas, and dog's tooth violet. These flowers can either be chosen to merge with the rest of the border or to dominate as bright patches of colour.

The shrubs with startlingly coloured stems – cornus and salix – can stand alone, but if you wish to surround them with bulbs, a covering of vivid yellow winter aconites will contrast with or complement their red or yellow stems before the leaves appear; alternatively pale narcissi could reflect the young leaves as they open.

Spring bulbs are the standbys for creating pools of colour wherever possible in the border, either at the edges or deep into the centre. I have white crocus down the middle of my borders, and on crisp, sunny days they make a fine display. As they develop and then die, their leaves are completely overlaid by the rising leaves of the herbaceous plants. *Iris reticulata* need to be seen close to, so position them on the corners of your borders among *Stachys lanata*, primulas, violas and *Campanula carpatica* or *C. garganica*. Early narcissi can be grown between aquilegias and the Kaufmanniana tulips among polyanthus. These bulbs can remain undisturbed and will spread naturally. I do urge you, however, not to make a solid carpet of startlingly coloured bulbs, but rather to interplant them with other emerging leaves to soften their primary colours and stiff, sometimes ungainly leaves into a tapestry woven with different greens.

Wallflowers and forget-me-nots are essential ingredients of a spring garden, however small. They can be liberally interplanted with tulips (daffodils are spent by the time the wallflowers and forget-me-nots are in full blow). Choose tulips with interesting shapes – those which are lily-flowered and those with fimbriated (frilly-edged) petals. Some of the double and semi-double varieties are exquisitely beautiful: 'Peach Blossom' is a deep rose colour, flushed white, and

'Angelique' a pastel pink. Both are double-flowered and more like soft-petalled peonies than stiff traditional tulips.

As soon as the flowers have faded the wallflowers and forget-me-nots, being biennials, will be taken out. At the same time you should take out the interplanted bulbs to store and reuse the following year. This creates an empty space in which to drop useful annuals, biennials or half-hardy plants to give a new look to your vases.

ANNUALS FOR LONG-LASTING COLOUR

Some gardeners scoff at annuals as parks department flowers but I think they have many virtues. They flower over several weeks, they come in all colours, they are frequently cut-and-come-again flowers, and most last well in water.

Annuals often have the advantage over perennials. The annual gypsophila is pure white and fast-growing; the perennial variety takes a year or two to settle down before it flowers. Similarly, although the perennial poppy *Papaver orientalis* is a wonderful border plant, it is the patch of annual Iceland poppies and *P. somniferum* 'Paeoniflorum' which stops me in my tracks. The new *P. somniferum* 'Hen and Chickens', which has tiny seed pods hanging around the main pod, is an original choice for a dried arrangement.

As well as the commonly grown annuals such as antirrhinums and petunias, broaden your repertoire to include cosmos, nemesias, cornflowers, clarkia, godetia and penstemon. Penstemon can be grown as an annual, although some of the perennial varieties, such as 'Garnet', 'Evelyn' and 'Hidcote Pink' do stand the winter or can be bought like annuals and introduced into a space.

The annuals can be wonderfully rich in colour. I love *Rudbeckia hirta* 'Rustic Dwarfs' in gold, brown and mahogany, and 'Marmalade' in rich golden-orange. They make a bold group in the garden and are excellent for picking. *Salvia farinacea* 'Victoria' has suitably regal purple spikes which look beautiful growing through grey-leaved *Senecio cineraria* 'Silver Dust'. Dahlias – not too tall or leafy – come in many special colours. I like the lesser known *D. merckii*, three feet (1m) high and an attractive pale mauve.

We all have our favourites – annuals we want to grow every year. Love-in-a-mist, *Nigella damascena*, is one of mine. It looks equally ravishing in the border and in a vase, where seed heads as well as flowers are useful. For early summer flowering, sow the seeds in containers in the autumn and mix them in between spring bulbs or polyanthus.

SPRING ESSENTIALS A blue carpet of forget-me-nots, interplanted with white tulips, can be removed when flowering is over and replaced with annuals, biennials or half-hardy plants for variety later in the year.

The half-hardy annuals are well worth working for. I use the Paris daisy, *Chrysanthemum frutescens*, in my borders as well as in containers. They flower profusely and their small, neat flowers are well suited to posies.

For constant flowering, the hybrid verbenas, *V*. 'Silver Ann' in pale pink and *V*. 'Sissinghurst' in bright pink, are successful space fillers. Put them between some perennials to intermingle. Very bright colours, like those of marigolds and nasturtiums, look better in an English light when softened by plenty of green and subtle shades of grey. Green is the linking factor throughout the garden.

INTRODUCING HEIGHT

The third dimension, which must be considered by the gardener, is height. There are several ways of introducing it immediately into the garden – with pergolas, arbours, fences and walls. Once the structure is there you can clothe it, using as many picking plants as possible. As you can make an interwoven pattern of plants on the ground, so you can create vertical pictures combining plants of different colours and textures to climb alongside and through one another.

Clematis and roses make ideal companions in colour, texture and compatability. If you are planting them to entwine with each other, pruning becomes easier if you choose a small-flowered clematis which flowers in the autumn on new wood and which needs to be cut hard back in spring, at the same time as the roses: the Viticella and Texensis groups and the lovely nodding yellow flowers of *C. tangutica*. The spring-flowering Alpina, Macropetala and Montana groups, all of which require very little pruning, are best given their own individual support, where they can form an intricate network and their seed heads can be left undisturbed to develop for autumn. The showy, large-flowered, summer-flowering clematis come in every colour. A few blooms, or even a single specimen, floating in a coloured glass bowl make a perfect centrepiece for a dinner party. In the garden they can climb up and through a winter-flowering shrub, such as *Garrya elliptica* or wintersweet, *Chimonanthus praecox*.

As for the climbing roses, bear in mind that a few – the white-flowered 'Kiftsgate', for instance – are multi-purpose for the flower arranger, providing flowers, scent and hips. I would concentrate, however, on those which have the two main attributes of colour and scent. The colours of roses are so exact these days that it is well worth your while spending time visiting rose nurseries and other rose collections to see the roses growing before you make your final choice of those that will suit your colour schemes in both garden and house.

'Mme Alfred Carrière', a noisette rose introduced in 1879 and often seen growing on old house walls, has large, strongly scented white blooms with a suspicion of pink. The thornless 'Zéphirine Drouhin' is a deep pink with a strong Bourbon scent; it flowers early and long and will do well on a north wall or near a doorway. Another white noisette I favour is 'Aimée Vibert', with small double flowers in large clusters; it is ideal for growing over arbours and arches.

If you are choosing yellow roses, 'Golden Showers' is fragrant, almost thornless, semi-double and long-flowering. The new hybrid 'Highfield' has proved a good introduction – it is yellow, highly scented and vigorous. Around your windows, doors or archways the scented 'Compassion' has the virtue of combining several shades, from light salmon pink to pale orange. For red I like 'Étoile de Hollande' and 'Fragrant Cloud'.

The vigorous ramblers are different in character, marvellous at enveloping your arbours but not quite so useful or long-lasting indoors.

THE THIRD DIMENSION *Roses and clematis, separately or together, are ideal for introducing height into the garden. The long-flowering rose 'Ispahan' (left) makes a fine backdrop for* Cistus *'Silver Pink'.* Clematis alpina *covers a wall (right) with delicate flowers in spring and silky seed heads later in the year.*

A WATER GARDEN

Water adds a whole new element to the garden and allows you to grow some water-loving plants you would not otherwise expect to see. The plants on the perimeter edge of this pool are all water-loving. On one side are the reds and on the other the yellows – primulas and astilbes – with hostas, ferns and grasses to cast their reflections in the water. A narrow brick pathway holds down the pool liner and gives access for picking. Beyond this path is a selection of shrubs to provide interest through the year.

Another path leads down to the pool and here two standards, *Buddleia alternifolia* and *Salix purpurea* 'Pendula', mark the way in. Hostas and shrubs provide greenery.

SPRING

PLANTING KEY

1 *Alchemilla mollis*
2 *Astilbe × arendsii* 'White Gloria'
3 *Corylus avellana* 'Contorta'
4 *Vinca major* 'Variegata'
5 *Syringa vulgaris* 'Madame Lemoine'
6 *Primula helodoxa*
7 *Glyceria spectabilis* 'Variegata'
8 *Ligularia dentata* 'Desdemona'
9 *Forsythia × intermedia* 'Lynwood'
10 *Hosta* 'Thomas Hogg'

11 *Filipendula ulmaria* 'Aurea'
12 *Spiraea × vanhouttei*
13 *Hosta* 'Gold Standard'
14 *Matteuccia struthiopteris*
15 *Spartium junceum*
16 *Polygonatum giganteum*
17 *Epimedium sulphureum*
18 *Caltha palustris*
19 *Viburnum plicatum* 'Mariesii'
20 Foxgloves (white)
21 *Primula florindae*
22 *Primula veris*
23 Muscari (blue, spring)
24 *Salix purpurea* 'Pendula' (standard)

25 *Iris sibirica*
26 Muscari (white, spring)
27 *Primula* 'Barnhaven'
28 *Buddleia alternifolia* (standard)
29 *Primula japonica*
30 Bronze fennel
31 *Stachys lanata*
32 *Ajuga pyramidalis* (spring)
33 *Thalictrum aquilegifolium*
34 Tulips (red, spring)
35 *Pittosporum* 'Garnettii'
36 *Lobelia cardinalis*
37 *Prunus × cistena* 'Crimson Dwarf'

38 *Aquilegia* 'Crimson Star'
39 *Salvia officinalis* 'Purpurascens'
40 *Iris laevigata* 'Snowdrift'
41 *Monarda* 'Cambridge Scarlet'
42 Lunaria
43 *Astilbe × arendsii* 'Fanal'
44 *Astrantia major*
45 *Hosta × tardiana* 'Halcyon'
46 *Penstemon* 'Garnet'
47 *Nepata × faassenii* 'Six Hills Giant'
48 *Rheum palmatum* 'Atropurpureum'

HIGH SUMMER

FLOWERS AND FOLIAGE FOR EVERY SEASON

In the garden, plants dictate their own span of life. Flowers are the most ephemeral, berries will endure until the birds find them, and leaves are part of the picture for the longest time. The gardener's art lies in marshalling these in a procession to last the year, creating a pattern of colour and texture that is continuously evolving.

As with everything in life, success lies in method. I cannot emphasize too much or too often how important it is to plan to have the material so that it is available in the necessary quantity and colours. To make the most of every month, I suggest that you make a chart of what you need and what will be available at each time of the year. Those people who use a computer can feed the information into it and then they will have an invaluable *aide-mémoire*, as long as the borders do not become 'planting by numbers'. You must always be flexible enough to buy and plant impulsively when you find a flower you know you would want to pick but which has not found its way into your list.

It is important to categorize your plants into trees, shrubs, herbaceous, annuals and bulbs as well as into colours, heights and times of use – this will be a great help when you come to plan where you are going to plant them.

IN THE DEPTHS OF WINTER

During the three months or so that winter lasts you will spend a great deal of time indoors, so it is logical to include as many winter-flowering plants as you can in your borders for picking. It is the small, special winter and early spring flowers you should grow, those rarely seen in the florist. It is a wonderful privilege in deep midwinter to go out with a basket and cut a few aconites to add to a flat bowl lined with fresh moss. You could pick a sprig of rosemary or *Hebe rakaiensis*, maybe a hellebore or two, and add a touch of grey with santolina leaves. The very action of going outside makes you aware of what is happening out there and will inspire you to put in more bulbs and other plants for winter picking.

I start my planning with that exciting and varied basket of flowers that can often be picked in England on Christmas Day or will be in flower soon after.

Think of the plants that include the words 'winter', 'Christmas' or 'snow' in their common names. Wintersweet (*Chimonanthus praecox*), winter honeysuckle (*Lonicera fragrantissima*) and winter jasmine (*Jasminum nudiflorum*) should all be in flower by mid-winter. The winter cherry or Chinese lantern is useful for a dried arrangement, and the irrepressible ground cover plant, *Gaultheria procumbens*, lives up to its common name of winter-green.

The first of the Christmas roses is *Helleborus niger*, and *Crataegus monogyna* 'Biflora', the Glastonbury thorn, miraculously always flowers in my garden on Christmas Day. For those with an acid soil, *Rhododendron* 'Christmas Cheer' should be in bloom. You can have snowdrops in flower all through the winter if you make a careful selection. Symphoricarpos, known in its green form as snowberry (*S. albus* var. *laevigatus*), is deciduous and has a generous supply of marble-like, glistening white berries. This shrub will sucker, so is only good for the larger garden, surviving even in shade and poor soil, but the pink-berried forms are more circumspect and good shrubs for odd corners.

The flowers you pick in the winter months have a special quality, perhaps because they have either survived the worst of the weather or have pushed through the cold soil because they are naturally winter-blooming. Some of these reluctant-to-die flowers had their heyday in the summer and autumn

FROST AND THAW *Silver needles of frost glistening on bare branches is always a handsome sight, but covering the twisted branches of a corkscrew hazel (*Corylus avellana contorta, *right) it is spectacular. Winter need not be just bare branches and frost: hellebores and the bright stems of* Cornus sibirica *(left) provide colour even before the first warm spell has enticed the first spring flowers into the open. They are a source of precious winter decoration both in the garden and indoors.*

but find the courage and stamina to hang on through the first frosts. As you walk round the garden you may well discover the last of the roses, low campanulas, some pansies, the occasional dianthus. These last are not to be counted on – they are a bonus for those who have eyes to find them – so should not come into your reckoning, but there are some reliable precocious blooms which push through whatever the weather, unless the ground is frozen hard. The earliest bulbs – chionodoxas, scillas and 'Peeping Tom' narcissus, and best of all the amazing *Iris unguicularis* – will always find a way. There are a wealth of hellebores opening, too, and the earliest polyanthus. I find that the pink pulmonaria, *Pulmonaria rubra*, comes into flower earlier than the common lungwort, *P. saccharata*, and the white *P. saccharata* 'Alba'.

A vase made only of leaves can be beautiful too. Once you start to pick them you will be amazed at how many different shades of green, gold and grey you can find. The evergreens that are the backbone of winter arrangements include holly,

27

euonymus, eucalyptus, eleagnus, privet and box. There are also some ferns, hebes and phillyrea. The long arms of the ivies and vincas are very useful for trailing at the base of vases – when ivies become arborescent they have clusters of black seed heads, useful and unusual for picking. The evergreen *Viburnum tinus* is perhaps one of the most rewarding of the shrubs, flowering from late autumn to early spring, and with its glossy dark leaves and pale pink flower heads it blends well in arrangements of all kinds. The previous year's shining blue-black fruits sometimes hang on long enough to combine with this year's flowers.

The evergreens are essential to keep the garden looking clothed and cared for in winter, but they are a bonus in summer as well. They can be used, *with discretion*, for cutting all through the year. By that I mean that you should never cut more than you need at one time and should always do your best to keep the tree or shrub shapely.

Seed heads and winter stems give a transparent feeling to the garden. Their structured outlines create subtle yet simple compositions lasting for many weeks indoors. It is especially important with these to choose an elegant and perhaps brightly coloured container. Seed heads which remain waiting to be picked from the border are *Phlomis viscosa* (*P. russeliana*), lunaria, clematis (especially *C. tangutica* and *C.* 'Bill Mackenzie'), many of the grass plumes and the brown heads of sedums and hydrangeas. To contrast with the seed heads or with living leaves and flowers there are the bright red, bulbous heads of *Iris foetidissima* and the equally bright, whip-like stems of salix and cornus.

Winter colours are mostly cool and subdued, harmonizing together, so it is important to consider shape in winter planning, setting spikes against soft mounds, seed heads of acanthus, eryngium and phlomis in contrast with soft evergreen hebes and phillyrea. Leaves may be spiky too: phormium and *Iris pallida* 'Variegata'. Hellebores to me epitomize winter – their sculptured forms need no other plant to promote their beauty.

SPRING BURSTS INTO COLOUR

After the subtlety of winter, the colours of spring enliven the garden but they require more careful planning as the available hues become brighter and more wide-ranging, matching the increasing length of daylight, the extra warmth in the sun and the eruption of plant life.

Flowering trees include prunus, malus, sorbus, cornus and magnolias in shades of white and of pink veering into red. They are colours which blend well in the garden and in the house, though most blossom lasts only long enough for a special occasion. Spring-flowering shrubs include willows for catkins, viburnums, pyracanthus, clematis (Alpinas,

Macropetalas and Montanas), osmanthus and rosemary.

Some shrubs will be opening yellow leaves – the golden variety of philadelphus, weigela, ligustrum, *Lonicera nitida* and eleagnus – and even the green leaves are more vibrant in their young growth. I like using golden-leaved shrubs together to create strong pools of light; they also make wonderful foils for spring bulbs like narcissi, daffodils, blue muscari, *Anemone blanda* and the later aquilegias.

I do not like bright yellows and reds together, so our red tulips have special homes, amongst dark evergreen shrubs, and in the shade of the laburnum walk before the yellow flowers open. The dappled shade of any deciduous trees brings out the strength of the reds, and they can be wonderful indoors, especially mixed with young green leaves. If you have the space, try them in meadow grass – they will remind you of poppy fields. I prefer to group both tulips and polyanthus by single colours, rather than mixing them. The tulips will have forget-me-nots growing with them, but the polyanthus should not be interplanted.

EXCITING SPRING HUES The clear, chartreuse-green of emerging hostas contrasting with bluebells (right), and the softer shades of white and mauve violas interspersed with pink-streaked tulips (below), show the range of spring colour. But the very wealth of choice makes it necessary to plan planting for picking very carefully.

SUMMER PROFUSION

With the fading of the spring flowers comes the excitement of changing the borders to their summer look. Half-hardy plants and annuals can be added where the tulips and forget-me-nots have been taken up, but it is the galaxy of colour among the perennials that will dominate your borders throughout the summer. Profusion is the key, and you must decide whether you want intense, electric colours or quieter, more pastel shades for your vases. Some flowers – delphiniums, lupins, rudbeckias, asters and dahlias – allow you to satisfy either inclination. Do not forget about white, which I like to use to punctuate or relieve the masses of bolder colours in my borders.

The richness of summer planting inspires large arrangements, often renewed, and encourages one to make the most of the dramatic spikes of delphiniums, hollyhocks, foxgloves and phlox. Roses, sweet peas and honeysuckles contribute fragrance. Shrubs in flower give extra weight, colour and interest to vases as they do in the garden.

Grey leaves are probably at their best in high summer when days are dry. My favourites are *Artemisia* 'Powis Castle', *Santolina incana*, and for a blue-grey, nepeta and rue.

As summer advances, so the first perennials will be spent and their untidy stems can be masked by later-flowering plants. Dahlias are in full bloom and the days of the asters just starting. Try and choose these after seeing them growing

RICH AUTUMNAL TINTS

Autumn can be one of the most beautiful times of the year in the garden, with berries ripening and the leaves of trees and shrubs turning to red, bronze and gold. It is easy to be carried away by the excitement of autumn colour. In a small garden try to choose a tree or shrub which combines spring blossom and autumnal leaves or berries. Make sure you choose appropriately for your soil. Acers and cercidiphyllum are amongst the best for leaf colour in an acid soil, and so are fothergilla, *Hamamelis mollis* and the yellow-berry or red forms of nandina. Prunus and malus will succeed in most soils, but in a garden with alkaline soil you should choose viburnums, sorbus, *Cotinus coggygria f. purpureus* and *Euonymus alata*.

In the border you can create a wonderful effect with hosta leaves, *Rudbeckia fulgida* 'Goldsturm' and kniphofia. *Lavatera olbia* 'Rosea' will continue flowering until the first frosts, and associates well with *Anemone japonica* and hydrangeas. Your roses will still be opening tenacious blooms. Soon the year will have come full circle and you will be thinking once more of flowers and foliage to pick for your cheering winter posies.

rather than from catalogues, so that you will be sure of the colour and the sturdy stems that will be less in need of staking. Now too, hardy chrysanthemums and physostegias are opening, and the spikes of acanthus standing tall.

ROSES AT SUMMER'S HEIGHT *Of all flowers, the rose (left and above) typifies the abundance of summer, contributing colour and fragrance which, with thoughtful planting, will enrich vases all summer long.*

AUTUMN JEWELS *The golden light of shortening days illuminates the rich oranges and browns of falling leaves and the intense burgundy-red heads of a clump of sedum.*

A Long, Sunny Border

This narrow border 11 yards (metres) long gets plenty of sun for a bright display. It is full of promise and picking material, where pale greys and whites, pinks and pale blues deepen in places to mauve and wine red. I have planned it without evergreen shrubs, except for a bush of rosemary and some greys in front, but evergreens could be easily substituted for some of the herbaceous plants.

At the back is a wall, fence or trellis – a sunspot clothed with roses, clematis, honeysuckles and a vine. The roots of the four clematis will be kept cool by the plants in front of them. The climbers are closely planted: I love seeing one plant embracing another, and what better combination than clematis and roses? Three of the clematis varieties flower in late summer, so they have been planted to grow with an early-flowering shrub. The wonderful rose 'Madame Plantier' flowers once, at the same time; her double cream blooms

AUTUMN

PLANTING KEY

AUTUMN

14 *Artemisia* 'Powis Castle'
15 *Solanum crispum* 'Glasnevin Var.'
16 *Philadelphus microphyllus*
17 *Nigella damascena*
18 *Molucella laevis*
19 Polyanthus
20 *Gypsophila paniculata* 'Rosy Veil'
21 *Sedum* 'Autumn Joy'
22 *Rosa* 'Madame Plantier'
23 *Clematis texensis* 'Gravetye Beauty'
24 Dahlias (pale pink and white)
25 *Tulipa* 'Angelique' or 'Apricot Beauty'
26 Rosemary
27 *Hosta × tardiana* 'Halcyon'

28 *Narcissus* 'Jack Snipe'
29 *Hebe pinguifolia*
30 *Narcissus* 'February Gold'
31 *Phlox canadensis*
32 *Syringa velutina* (*palibiniana*)
33 *Lonicera japonica repens* (*flexuosa*)
34 *Clematis* 'Marie Boisselot'
35 *Aster novae-angliae* 'Harrington's Pink'
36 *Scabiosa caucasica* 'Clive Greaves'
37 Scilla or chionodoxa
38 *Narcissus* 'February Silver'
39 *Narcissus* 'Jenny'
40 *Vitis vinifera* 'Purpurea'
41 *Clematis viticella* 'Alba Luxurians'

1 *Tulipa* 'White Triumphator'
2 *Diascia rigescens*
3 *Nepeta mussinii*
4 *Iris reticulata*
5 Acanthus
6 *Narcissus* 'Mary Copeland'
7 *Rosa* 'Blomfield Abundance'
8 *Kolkwitzia amabilis*
9 *Clematis* 'Huldine'
10 *Monarda* 'Prairie Night'
11 Agapanthus
12 *Santolina incana*
13 *Stachys lanata*

have a green eye, and she acts as host to *Clematis* 'Gravetye Beauty'. *Kolkwitzia amabilis*, with soft pink flowers and interesting seed heads, has *Clematis* 'Huldine' as its partner to flower later. This clematis has a surprising beauty when it is picked; its white petals are shot through with a central green line. Beneath the climbers, daffodils create splashes of yellow through the border in spring.

In the central strip which runs along the length of the border, are many other bulbs – tulips, narcissi, scillas, chionodoxas and *Iris reticulata*. Starting on the left comes the lily-flowered *Tulipa* 'White Triumphator', which I then dig up and store, replacing them for the summer with *Diascia rigescens*. *Narcissus* 'Mary Copeland' come through the acanthus, and *Iris reticulata* through *Nepeta mussinii*. Hosta leaves spread themselves later in the year, so there is always space around them for early-flowering daffodils like 'Jack Snipe' and 'February Gold'. I hate to be without forget-me-nots in the borders and for picking. To go with them I have chosen *Tulipa* 'Angelique' or 'Apricot Beauty'. If the quantity is doubled, it is possible to have enough to pick without spoiling the effect in the border. I would sow some hardy annuals in this border in the autumn; they often come through the winter and make especially good plants.

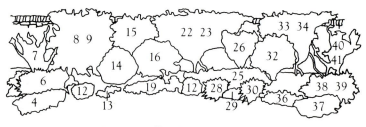

EARLY SPRING

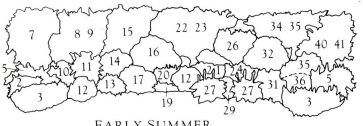

EARLY SUMMER

34

EARLY SPRING

EARLY SUMMER

MAKING THE MOST OF PROBLEM AREAS

No garden is without its problem areas, but there are ways of making the most of them. A common difficulty is a bed that has too much shade, caused by a high wall or hedge, or by the overhanging branches of a tree. If a shaded border is backed by a wall, you will discover that in winter it gets really no sun at all. This means that frost will persist much longer there, but to compensate, the light intensity will be higher than under a thick conifer, and there will be no competition from tree roots, so the soil will not be too dry.

If the border lies underneath a beautiful deciduous tree, you can increase the amount of light it receives by thinning the branches overall and by removing some of the lower branches completely. Trees with large leaves create dense shade; others with finer leaves, like gleditsias and rowans, allow some light to filter through.

Plants that will grow in the dry shade created by trees include alchemilla, aucuba, bamboos, bergenia, epimedium, *Euonymus fortunei*, various hollies, *Iris foetidissima*, ivies, liriope, pachyphragma, skimmia, symphoricarpos and vinca. These are mostly foliage plants, so choose several with variegated leaves and position them for texture as well as size.

There is a greater choice of flowers for a shady bed with less dry soil – one under a north-facing wall. You can add astilbe, camellia, fothergilla, gaultheria, polygonum, and *Viburnum opulus* to the list above. Among climbers that will grow happily against a shady wall are chaenomeles, cotoneaster, forsythia, *Garrya elliptica*, *Hydrangea petiolaris*, *Jasminum nudiflorum*, *Kerria japonica*, *Schizophragma hydrangeoides*. Some of the clematis flowers – 'Lord Northcliffe' and 'Nellie Moser', for example – fade less in shade. Climbing roses which will do well here include 'Mme Alfred Carrière', 'Zéphirine Drouhin', 'Gloire de Dijon', 'Gloire de Ducher', 'Albéric Barbier', 'Mermaid', 'Blairi No. 2', and 'Souvenir de Mme Léonie Viennot'. The Albas, Rugosas and Gallicas all tolerate poor soil in partial shade, and so can form part of the shaded border.

A really sun-baked border needs as much care in the selection of its plants as one in deep shadow. Think of the plants you associate with hot Mediterranean climates when choosing. Shrubs can include artemisia, brooms, caryopteris, cistus, helichrysum, hibiscus, hippophae, rosemary, salvia, tamarisk, yucca. For perennials choose acanthus, alstroemeria, crocosmia, dianthus, echinops, eryngium, kniphofia, nerine, poppies, verbascum.

Seaside gardens present a particular problem because of wind and salt-laden air. In a new garden the priority is for shelter. A young hedge will itself need protection, so a wall or fence is much the best solution if you can afford one. Shrubs which will withstand salt air and wind include those with narrow or grey leaves – *Atriplex halimus* or tree purslane, *Elaeagnus* × *ebbingei*, genista, griselinia, *Hebe salicifolia*, lavender, *Olearia* × *haastii*, rosemary, *Rosa pimpinellifolia*, *Senecio* 'Sunshine' and tamarisk. Most of these will also do well on exposed, windy sites inland.

CONDITIONS UNDER FOOT

Soil type may cause your biggest headache, whether it is heavy clay, chalk or stony ground. In each case, it will improve if you keep working on it and enriching it.

Clay is unmistakable – heavy, sticky and toffee-coloured – and at first glance you may think it is unworkable. Bear in mind, though, that it is rich in plant food, retained in the soil for a long time because of these very characteristics. To help break down the clay, add as much organic matter as possible, and keep on doing so. It will make digging easier, darken the soil and generally improve the drainage. All this added material – farmyard manure, mushroom compost, peat and garden compost – may mean that you can create some raised beds: a change of level, especially in a small garden, creates extra interest and incident.

Shrubs that thrive on clay soil are aralia, choisya, forsythia, hamamelis, lilac and two viburnums – *V. tinus* and *V. plicatum*. For perennials you might have camassia, digitalis, helenium, *Narcissus cyclamineus* and *N. bulbocodium*, *N.* 'Golden Harvest' and *N.* 'Mount Hood', and sunflowers.

Roses also do well on clay, and a feature of a garden with clay soil could be a rose hedge using *R. rugosa* 'Blanc Double de Coubert' or 'Roseraie de L'Hay' for a tall hedge, *R. gallica* 'Versicolor' or *R.* 'Buff Beauty' for a medium hedge, and 'Old Blush China' or 'Little White Pet' for a small hedge.

Chalk, also a problem, requires much the same treatment as clay. Leaf mould and mulch are particularly helpful for enriching a shallow chalky topsoil. Each time you put in a shrub, make a good-sized planting hole and fill it with compost, integrating this into the surrounding chalk. Box, choisya, clematis, daphne, deutzia, *Hydrangea villosa*, kolkwitzia, and potentilla are all suitable shrubs for this type of soil. Dianthus, bearded irises, peonies, and scabious could be included among the perennials.

Stony ground is more of a bore than a problem. Stones are not easy to remove, but you should take them off the surface, if only to improve the appearance of your borders. Once again, keep adding organic matter, especially farmyard manure and your own garden compost. The soil will be well drained, so you can make your choise from among those plants which appreciate such conditions – shrubs such as cytisus, genista, perovskia, rosemary and phlomis, and perennials like acanthus, asphodels, bergenia, eryngium, hardy geraniums and thalictrum.

COVERING AN EYESORE

A different and difficult problem can be covering an ugly shed or outbuilding. Rampant climbing roses are often the answer and wire netting tied over the roof provides the roses with a means of climbing. Choose a rambler such as *Rosa*

TOLERANT OF CHALK *Bearded irises, their ruffled heads belying their stately demeanour (above), are among many perennials that will tolerate chalky soil.*

WOODLAND SHADE *Foxgloves and hostas thrive in a patch of moist shade under trees close to a river bank (left), but both will also do well in much dryer shade.*

filipes 'Kiftsgate', *R.* 'Bobbie James' or *R.* 'Paul's Himalayan Musk'. Their huge panicles of flowers will bring scent indoors when you pick them. They will all grow to 30ft (10m) and more and fortunately pruning is not essential.

The best clematis for this situation are *C. montana* or *C. armandii* – neither needs pruning. Honeysuckles are also good, especially the early Dutch *Lonicera periclymenum* 'Belgica' and the later-flowering *L. periclymenum* 'Serotina'. For a shady place you could choose the vine *Parthenocissus henryana*, which climbs by adhesive pads so requires no extra support. The leaves are good for picking at all times and they turn a magnificent red in autumn before they fall.

The Russian vine, *Polygonum baldschuanicum*, sometimes called the 'mile-a-minute' vine because it grows so fast, will quickly cover a roof. It is very striking from the middle of summer through to autumn when its panicles of white flowers are abundant and will look glorious in a vase.

A LONG, SHADY BORDER

I first thought – since it gets little sun – that this border, 11 yards (metres) long and designed for autumn, winter and spring, could be quite a problem, but when I started to plan it there was almost a surfeit of plants to include. In spite of having only a few evergreens it is full of interest.

A shady border presents an exciting challenge. I have tried to keep it to white, pale yellow, blues and greens from the darkest through to lime. It is a place where you could try out startling combinations – *Erysimum* 'Bowles' Purple' in front of a group of *Euphorbia characias*, perhaps, or *Helleborus corsicus* with a very dark purple honesty. I always leave the honesty heads on to form their lovely silver 'pennies'.

Against the back wall or fence are two ivies, *Hedera helix* 'Glacier' and *H. colchica* 'Paddy's Pride', the latter interwoven with *Clematis* 'Jackmanii Superba'. *C. tangutica* is planted beside *Garrya elliptica* and should be encouraged to climb through it. The seed heads of the clematis look lovely in company with the tassels of the garrya both in the garden and in a vase. *Rosa* 'Mermaid' and *Clematis* 'Perle d'Azur' make another good combination. The winter standby *Jasminum nudiflorum* must be given a good place where it will be clearly seen and so must a pyracantha and a cotoneaster. The rather delicate rose 'Madame Alfred Carrière' I find actually does better in shade than in full sun; since she only

EARLY AUTUMN

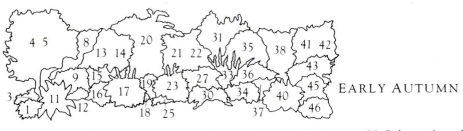

EARLY AUTUMN

PLANTING KEY

1 *Helleborus orientalis*
2 Snowdrops
3 Pulmonaria
4 *Hedera helix* 'Glacier'
5 *Prunus mume*
6 *Scilla* 'Spring Beauty'
7 Muscari
8 *Jasminum nudiflorum*
9 Aquilegia
10 *Narcissus* 'Mount Hood'
11 *Polystichum setiferum*
12 Violas

13 *Rosa* 'Mermaid'
14 *Clematis* 'Perle d'Azur'
15 *Lunaria biennis* 'Variegata'
16 *Campanula muralis* (*portenschlagiana*)
17 *Hosta sieboldiana*
18 *Viola cornuta*
19 Epimedium
20 *Cotoneaster salicifolius*
21 *Hedera colchica* 'Paddy's Pride'
22 *Clematis* 'Jackmanii Superba'
23 *Hosta* 'Gold Standard'

24 *Narcissus* 'Spellbinder'
25 Ajuga (bronze)
26 *Iris reticulata*
27 Astrantia
28 *Narcissus* 'Trevithian'
29 Primulas
30 Nasturtiums
31 *Pyracantha* 'Mojave'
32 *Narcissus* 'Cheerfulness'
33 *Digitalis × mertonensis*
34 *Tiarella cordifolia*
35 *Garrya elliptica*

36 Solomon's seal
37 *Euphorbia polychroma*
38 *Clematis tangutica*
39 *Helleborus foetidus*
40 *Hosta* 'Frances Williams'
41 *Rosa* 'Madame Alfred Carrière'
42 *Clematis viticella* 'Abundance'
43 *Mahonia ×* 'Charity'
44 *Narcissus* 'Thalia'
45 *Nicotiana affinis* (white)
46 Bergenia

flowers once, there is an autumn clematis climbing through her and *Mahonia* × 'Charity' in front. Hellebores, hostas and Solomon's seal thrive in this shady border – all make larger clumps over the years, so I include a biennial such as honesty around them initially so that there are no gaps when they are still quite small.

As this is primarily a winter and spring bed I use bulbs in abundance: snowdrops, muscari, scillas and narcissi. Amongst the narcissi I plant aquilegias and foxgloves. If the bulbs are left alone for a year or two they will increase, giving plenty of flowers to cut. The smaller bulbs do well under *Prunus mume*, the Japanese apricot, which blooms in late winter. Here is a suitable place for ferns and the large-leaved bergenias, which give lovely foliage for use in vases.

Low plants with lovely small flowers for posies make the most of the long front. Blue ajuga flowers with yellow *Euphorbia polychroma*, and *Tiarella cordifolia* with hellebore seed heads make an interesting arrangement. *Narcissus* 'Thalia' are taken out after they have flowered and are replaced by white *Nicotiana affinis*, *Begonia* 'Thousand Wonders White' or white busy lizzies.

For planting key, see previous page.

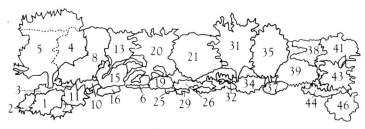

WINTER

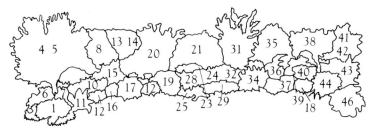

SPRING

WINTER

SPRING

AN ARTIST'S PALETTE OF COLOUR

When you walk round certain gardens, where the colours, textures, shapes and sizes all have an underlying harmony, you know at once that the owner is an artist. Flower arranging calls for much the same sensitivity – an appreciation of detail and an eye for colour – but fortunately it is a talent which is not confined, as it is in painting, to the gifted few: it can be developed through observation and practice.

There is a subtle difference between the colour of flowers in the garden and indoors. This is owing to the intensity of light, the distance from which they are seen, and the predominance of green in the garden compared to the relative importance of other colours in the house.

Daytime light is always brighter in the garden. The stronger the sunlight, the more assertive the hot colours – red, orange, yellow – will appear. Material or clothes bought in a country where the light is vibrant can often be much too startling to use or wear in the more diluted English light. The same is true of certain plants – think of scarlet hibiscus, red and purple bougainvillea or bright red geraniums, all of which make tricky companions in a northern garden.

In the house, incandescent electric light, replacing natural light, gives everything a yellow cast – creamy colours become more golden, and blues tend towards green unless they have purple in them, when they become much darker. Mauves deepen too, but reds, if they are on the orange side, become brighter. Experiment with these colours yourself: arrange a vase during daylight to match or blend with a chosen feature – china or chintz – then draw the curtains and see how the colour alters under electric light. If you have dimmer switches in your rooms, you will notice that flowers with red and yellow in their make-up become more intense as you turn the light up. Others – blues, purples, browns and pinks – become darker. It is a curious phenomenon that if you know the colour of a flower – a scarlet Oriental poppy, for instance – your eye and your memory will continue to tell you its true colour when you see it in artificial light, whereas a person who does not have your knowledge will see it as it appears under electric light.

Candle-light is as flattering to flowers as it is to faces, so use candles on the dining-room table whenever you can, letting the soft light play directly on to the flower arrangement. Not only will the flickering candle flame add life to each bloom, but the shadows on the petals will be constantly deepening and shifting. If you revolve a small vase on the table, different parts of the arrangement will be highlighted in turn and you will notice how the pattern of dominance in the colours varies. Try this with *Geranium* 'Johnson's Blue' and *Alchemilla mollis*, with the pink *Verbena* 'Sissinghurst' and any white flower, with nepeta and golden leaves. In each case green may be included as infill and will tie the colours together, as it does in the garden.

COLOUR CHANGING WITH THE MONTHS

I associate each season with a particular colour range. Spring with its galaxy of bulbs includes white through cream to deep yellow, blue and purple. The useful grey foliage plants have not yet come into their own, so the colours tend to appear fresh rather than soft, an effect heightened by the citrus green of the opening leaves and emerging perennials. I generally limit the use of reds during this season, although I love the deep velvet crimson of the Barnhaven primulas and use them in bold groups, keeping otherwise to an occasional flash of scarlet tulips, not a whole swathe.

It is during the summer that the hot colours come into their own, but even then they are toned down by the volume of greens – in lawns and trees as well as in the border foliage. There are crimson peonies to pick, poppies, kniphofias, dahlias, marigolds, alstroemerias, asters, and both annual and perennial rudbeckias. Roses range from bright reds and yellows through pinks to peach and white.

In the garden I like to mix my summer blues and mauves with lemon and deeper yellows: campanulas, violas, delphiniums, *Polemonium caeruleum*, *Thalictrum aquilegifolium*, scabious, nepeta and nigella to merge with *Anthemis tinctoria*, *Alchemilla mollis* and the golden leaves of hostas, *Philadelphus coronarius* 'Aureus' and *Ligustrum ovalifolium* 'Aureum'. These colours may be held together by grey leaves: *Artemisia* 'Powis Castle', santolina and *Stachys lanata*, lavender, *Teucrium fruticans* and the curry plant, *Helichrysum angustifolium*. White roses, lilies, nicotiana, gypsophila, *Galtonia candicans* and the white flowers of *Hosta* 'Royal

REFLECTIONS OF SUN AND SKY *Yellows and blues appear in the garden through both spring and summer, but the impression is very different. Early in the year, there is little to challenge the heavy gold of daffodils and equally intense muscari blue (left), but later, now the volume of green is at its peak, colours just as strong appear softer and more harmonious (above).*

Standard' can be used amongst the blues and yellows and sometimes act as a substitute for the grey leaves.

With the approach of autumn, green becomes less dominant in the garden, as the leaves on the deciduous trees and shrubs change colour and finally drop. Colour among the evergreens often darkens, too, and in your planting you can reflect the emergence of a colour range dominated by reds which are mellower than in summer and mixed with bronze, dark or rusty orange and deep yellow. It is the only time of the year that I enjoy combining red and yellow – the red has lost some of its glare and the yellow foliage usually has a tinge of orange, with some trees like liquidambar and parrotia combining all these colours in a single leaf.

In the border choose those shades which underline the changing mood of the garden, planting the deep bronze chrysanthemums in preference to the paler strains, and purple as well as golden rudbeckias. Brought indoors, they will glow in the firelight and reflect the amber of the beech leaves gathered in the woods and dried under the carpet.

In winter the starkness of the bare earth and the branches silhouetted black against grey skies or snow can create a greater uniformity of colour in the garden. This background generates a different mood, and the flowers on the shrubs will stand out well even though they are small and not brightly coloured. There are viburnums, ericas, wintersweet and winter honeysuckles to enjoy, and mahonia and *Daphne mezereum* starting to open. These have neat, more waxy blooms, whose delicacy comes home to you as you are cutting them to bring indoors. You will appreciate their scents, which will strengthen in the warmth of your rooms. The elusive nature of winter colour is evident, too, in the berries – as the weather gets more bitter they will start to disappear as the birds devour them.

RESTRICTING THE SPECTRUM

In a small garden where almost everything is visible at a glance I think it is best to keep the colours to a certain side of the spectrum for each season. This may mean that you will have to sacrifice some flowers which do not fit into your colour range. In a larger garden made up of outdoor rooms or compartments, or in a long, narrow garden which you may wish to divide into two or three, you can follow Lawrence Johnston's practice at Hidcote of having red borders and Vita Sackville-West's idea of a white garden at Sissinghurst. Gertrude Jekyll wrote about the golden, the blue and the green garden. You must rely on your instinct about your own garden; in so doing you will discover how colours influence one another, creating vibrating, calming or even melancholy combinations and effects.

In a red border, blue-red flowers, I have discovered, do not go well with orange-red ones. When it is the foliage that is red, however, this does not seem to matter. Grey looks better than pure white with red, and if you find that a particular shade of red is too strong for your border, the way to soften it is not with white flowers but by adding a more diluted or a deeper version of the same red.

When you study the white flowers in your garden, and even more so if you copy, as many people have copied, Vita Sackville-West's white garden, you will discover how many whites there are, how they cool down the garden and how the flowers contrast with the grey, green and golden foliage.

Few flowers are totally white – they will have a tinge or a streak of another colour. You can emphasise this secondary colour in the flowers you choose to pick. Snowdrops have green markings, *Clematis* 'Miss Bateman' has chocolate-coloured instead of the more usual yellow stamens, and *Lilium regale*, one of the easiest lilies to grow, has a sulphur yellow centre. The grey-white flowers of *Lysimachia ephemerum* contrast perfectly with their grey-green foliage. Add an element of blue amongst the whites and this will heighten the effect of the grey leaves.

Many leaves have white or cream margins or veining. *Arum italicum* 'Pictum' is invaluable from autumn until spring, when the leaves die down. The handsome-leaved *Brunnera macrophylla* 'Variegata' is also splashed with cream, and the foliage of the ornamental strawberry *Fragaria × ananassa* 'Variegata', so useful in arrangements, has a striking effect in the garden. Remember that white stands out, becoming almost luminous, as the evening light fades.

GOLD AND SILVER *A garden created around white flowers can never be wholly white and the mood will differ with the colouring of the other flowers and foliage. Yellow and gold (below) contribute an exuberant, sunny element. With silver and grey-green foliage (right), a more restful and contemplative mood settles on the garden.*

Think of texture in relation to colour as well: a diffuse genista in flower works well near a solid yellow-leaved shrub such as *Philadelphus coronarius* 'Aureus'. Hostas with yellow leaves can complement *Potentilla* 'Elizabeth', golden daisy-flowers, *Anthemis tinctoria*, *Helianthus* 'Loddon Gold' and *Coreopsis verticillata* 'Moonbeam'. Golden-leaved conifers are popular, but they become very dominant in the garden and I personally do not like them in arrangements, except in the winter as infilling in a flat vase.

For a lightness of texture and as a contrast to pure golden leaves, consider including plants with yellow variegation on their leaves, from the grasses, such as *Molinia caerulea* 'Variegata' or the attractive bamboo *Arundinaria viridistriata*, through to *Cornus alba* 'Spaethii', *Elaeagnus pungens* 'Maculata' and the variegated forms of euonymus, holly and box.

A blue garden is easier to create than a golden one, as long as you keep the purple shades away from the bright blues such as forget-me-nots and some of the delphiniums. Purple-blues include *Iris sibirica*, lavender, violet-blue lupins, *Campanula glomerata* 'Superba' and *C. persicifolia*, *Centaurea dealbata* 'John Coutts' and nepeta. Blue agapanthus look best growing through grey foliage – I use *Artemisia ludoviciana* and *A.* 'Powis Castle'. The eryngiums are all good for cutting: those with a silvery tinge mix with anything, while those whose colour is a more metallic blue go better with brighter blues such as *Delphinium* 'Blue Jay'.

Throughout history all-green gardens have been created, using topiary, pattern and texture to take the place of colour. Such a planting is restful to look at and walk in, and can be as satisfying as a riot of colour. In my gardening life, I have discovered that there is less discordance of colour the more you simplify. This applies in your house as well, and it is a thought I keep in the front of my mind whenever I embark on a new planting scheme.

The colour of plants is closely linked to their texture. The leaves of choisya, aucuba and holly glow green largely because they are glossy and waxy. Compare them to alchemilla leaves; their blotting-paper texture turns them a uniform shade, saved from dullness by their delicately sculptured shape. The hairy surface of many grey-leaved plants makes them woolly to the touch and is an essential part of their soft greyness, in the same way that velvet is rendered velvety as much by the feel of its nap as by its rich, jewel-like colouring. Learning how to blend or graduate textures is as important as learning how to achieve a balance of colours.

In the garden, plants have no competitors, apart perhaps from a few brightly dressed humans, a striped awning or a turquoise chlorinated swimming pool – flowers and leaves supply all the colour you see. In the house it is a very different

A predominantly white garden works well, but not a totally golden one. A border filled with golden flowers and foliage can be most striking, glinting in the sun, especially if it is south-facing, but it must be carefully conceived, and it must have touches of grey, blue or purple. Keep away from reds and pinks. The other colours must be placed to bring out but not to detract from the yellow: a purplish-leaved holly should be partially obscured by golden-leaved shrubs, but a holly with a yellow variegation – *Ilex × attaclarensis* 'Lawsoniana' perhaps – can be given a more important place. Before planting, try to match your colours together; if two yellows tend to kill one another, they should be kept apart, using grey or a paler shade of yellow between them. I have *Lonicera nitida* 'Baggesen's Gold' underplanted with golden marjoram, but with a dividing strip of bergenia.

story. Flower arrangements have to do what they can to stand out among the colourful wallpapers, fabrics, ornaments and paintings vying for attention in every room. Flower arrangers usually think of blending flowers with fabrics, but I would like you to think of your rooms and *all* the elements in your decoration schemes. Perhaps for a change you could pick out the colours of a favourite picture or ornament, reflect in your study the shades of the book bindings, or match in your kitchen the bright colours of saucepans and containers. The attention of your guests will be turned, not to your curtains and sofa, but to your favourite possessions.

With all the colour competition indoors, it is no wonder that in large arrangements the showy single flowers of roses, peonies and rhododendrons take pride of place, and that these too are the candidates for placing singly in a vase. This brings me to the greatest difference between flowers in the house and in the garden: their proximity. By and large in the garden you are more aware of plants as coloured masses than as individuals. Often visitors say to me, 'How full of colour the garden is' – they are only aware of the effect and do not take in the details. Curiously enough, they seem to have a blind spot towards green, taking it for granted. The same plants, when brought indoors, have every element heightened because they are made a focus of attention. The variegation in every leaf, the shading in every petal, demand admiration. This is the biggest bonus of all.

As beautiful as flower arrangements can be, for me one of the simplest and most satisfying effects is created by picking a leaf here, a flower head there and arranging them at random in a shallow bowl on a table where they can be studied close to. You may be sure that whatever colours you pick, if your garden is in harmony there will never be a note of disharmony in that informal cluster. Most important of all, you will be learning gradually and effortlessly two of the fundamental lessons of both gardening and flower arranging – an intimate friendship with the plants in your garden, and the endless permutation of textures and colours that will open your eyes to new possibilities for planning and planting.

MUTED SHADES *Some of the softest tones in the gardener's palette lie in the lavender/pink area of the spectrum. Chive flowers, aquilegia and* Clematis *'Nelly Moser' (left) elegantly reflect each other in an informal garden.*

CONTRAST AND COMPLEMENT *Startling clashes of colour have their place in the garden as much as subtle harmonies. Glowing pink tulips (top) intensify purple and lilac violas. Flowers of the same hue but different strength – peonies and* Kolkwitzia amabilis *– enhance each other (centre). A simple but effective contrast is created with* Nigella damascena *and scarlet* Papaver rhoeas *'Ladybird' (right).*

47

AN ISLAND BED PLANTED WITH COOL COLOURS

This kidney-shaped island bed, 9 yards (metres) long, is filled with cool colours chiefly planned to yield spring and summer flowers. Inevitably it also includes evergreens – I always find it hard not to use them in my planting.

When I have drawn out the shape of the border, I select and place the bushes. Here there are five: the evergreen *Osmanthus delavayi*, with its small but shining green leaves; the silver-splashed form of *Ligustrum ovalifolium*; and three deciduous flowering shrubs – philadelphus, kolkwitzia and *Viburnum plicatum*. You could substitute a blue-flowered hibiscus for one of these, but it is not as reliable or as useful in arrangements.

I then make a choice of plants to go round the edge of my border. On the shady side are hellebores, ferns, bergenias and pulmonarias. Ideally it should be the sunny side which you can see from the house or from the main sitting-out place, as that has plenty of summer colour. Here are nigella and dianthus, bold hosta leaves in several varieties and crimson antirrhinums. *Campanula persicifolia* stand tall behind *Scabiosa caucasica* 'Clive Greaves' and nigellas, and *Stachys lanata* are backed by agapanthus. Delphinium spikes push between the central shrubs and acanthus makes a bold impact behind the hostas and dianthus.

Spring bulbs, planted throughout this border, create a feeling of fullness and provide plenty of cutting material.

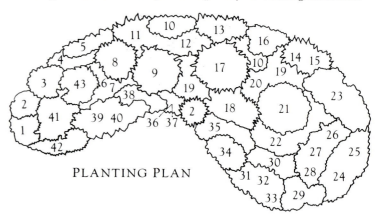

PLANTING PLAN

SPRING

PLANTING KEY

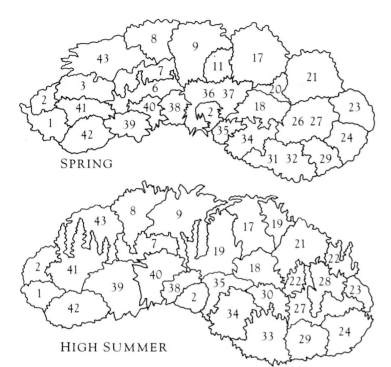

SPRING

HIGH SUMMER

1 *Saxifraga × urbium*
2 *Santolina incana*
3 *Helleborus foetidus*
4 *Muscari armeniacum*
5 *Epimedium sulphureum*
6 *Tulipa* 'West Point' (yellow)
7 Lunaria (white)
8 *Ligustrum ovalifolium* 'Argenteum'
9 *Philadelphus* 'Belle Etoile'
10 *Pulmonaria saccharata* 'Argentea'
11 *Tulipa* 'White Triumphator'
12 *Chrysanthemum maximum*
13 *Polystichum setiferum*
14 Dryopteris
15 *Asplenium scolopendrium*
16 *Helleborus orientalis*
17 *Kolkwitzia amabilis*
18 *Agapanthus* 'Headbourne Hybrids'
19 Delphinium
20 *Tulipa* 'Mariette' (pink)
21 *Osmanthus delavayi*

22 *Campanula persicifolia*
23 *Bergenia cordifolia* 'Purpurea'
24 *Nepeta mussinii*
25 Puschkinia
26 *Narcissus* 'Flower Record'
27 Aquilegia
28 *Lilium candidum*
29 *Sedum* 'Autumn Joy'
30 *Scabiosa caucasica* 'Clive Greaves'
31 *Scilla siberica*
32 *Primula* 'Barnhaven'
33 Antirrhinum (crimson)
34 *Stachys lanata*
35 *Nigella damascena*
36 *Narcissus* 'Trevithian'
37 *Narcissus* 'Mount Hood'
38 *Euphorbia polychroma*
39 *Hosta* 'Frances Williams'
40 *Hosta fortunei* 'Aurea'
41 *Acanthus spinosus*
42 Dianthus
43 *Viburnum plicatum* 'Mariesii'

HIGH SUMMER

AN ISLAND BED PLANTED WITH HOT COLOURS

I have chosen shrubs with golden and green foliage as the back-bone of this oval-shaped island bed, 5 yards (metres) by 3½ yards (metres). The evergreens, *Hebe rakaiensis*, *Ilex × altaclarensis* 'Lawsoniana', *Euonymus fortunei* 'Emerald and Gold', and the bamboo *Arundinaria viridistriata* last for weeks in water and the golden privet, *Ligustrum ovalifolium* 'Aureum', is useful for cutting through the year unless the winter is severe. These shrubs punctuate the bed in winter, and for summer there are wonderfully scented white philadelphus, and the spectacular *Spiraea × bumalda* 'Goldflame' with leaves mixed gold and red. There are two roses for picking, one red and the other white.

The infilling between these anchor plants consists of hardy perennials, a few annuals and some spring bulbs. The colours range from bright reds to oranges and yellows, with the reds on the yellow side of the spectrum. I have added some greys to hold the colour together.

This border will look good in spring with young leaves showing and under-planted with bulbs, but its main time for picking will be summer and autumn.

HIGH SUMMER

PLANTING KEY

1 *Coreopsis auriculata* 'Superba'
2 Poppies (orange-red)
3 *Artemisia* 'Powis Castle'
4 *Spiraea × bumalda* 'Goldflame'
5 Zinnias
6 *Ligustrum ovalifolium* 'Aureum'
7 Pot marigolds
8 Golden marjoram
9 Dahlias (orange-red)
10 Dahlias (white)
11 *Hebe rakaiensis*
12 *Viola cornuta* 'Alba'
13 Rose (red floribunda)
14 *Anaphilis triplinervis*
15 *Hosta* 'Gold Standard'
16 *Crocosmia × crocosmiiflora* 'Emily McKenzie'
17 Lunaria (deep mauve)
18 *Gaillardia* 'Mandarin'
19 Alstroemeria
20 *Ilex × altaclarensis* 'Lawsoniana'
21 *Euonymus fortunei* 'Emerald and Gold'
22 *Rosa* 'Iceberg'
23 *Viola cornuta* 'Belmont Blue'
24 *Arundinaria viridistriata*
25 *Philadelphus microphyllus*
26 Nasturtiums (trailing)
27 *Anthemis tinctoria*
28 *Rudbeckia hirta* 'Marmalade'
29 *Hosta* 'Frances Williams'

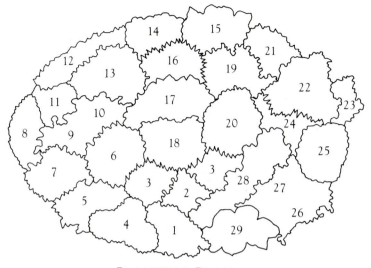

PLANTING PLAN

AUTUMN

HERBS AMONG THE FLOWER BEDS

Fresh herbs, just picked for cooking, are one of the delights of a garden, but they also make an unusual addition to vases: parsley, fennel, sage and thyme for small posies, lovage and angelica for bolder effects. Herb gardens create a romantic picture in summer, but they must have a firm, well-tutored design if they are to remain attractive in winter. If you do not wish to give over space to a separate herb garden, most of the herbs you will want to use in the kitchen will fit easily into your borders alongside the flowers and shrubs.

Angelica, towering up to six feet (2m), is one of the stateliest of the taller perennial and biennial herbs. The flower and seed heads are wonderful in an arrangement. Do not plant them too far back in the border – you should be able to reach them easily to remove the seed heads before they scatter too many seeds around. Elecampane (*Inula helenium*) and lovage are six-footers too. Elecampane has huge leaves and shaggy yellow, late-summer flowers rather like sunflowers. I have it growing behind a golden-leaved privet and the two yellows complement each other. The young growth of lovage is crimson, attractive in the garden and unusual in an early-summer vase.

Fennel is indispensable both for flavour and for its feathery foliage which is either green or a wonderful bronze. It mixes well with almost every plant in the garden and contributes to the border all summer. If you allow it to seed itself you will find it coming up in a magical manner amongst other perennials. The leaves do not last for long in water but give an impressive, rather airy effect while they are fresh.

There is a good selection of lower-growing, hardy perennial herbs. The late summer-flowering bergamot has interesting, scented leaves and flowers ranging from pink to deepish mauve. Foxgloves are useful as infillers, and so too are dame's violets, *Hesperis matronalis*, with sprays of white or lilac flowers sweet-smelling in the evening.

Several of the herb sub-shrubs are essential near the front of a border. They include lavender, sage, rosemary, santolina and southernwood, *Artemisia abrotanum*. The traditional plant to put under roses is *Nepeta × faassenii*, and this combines well with lavender. Plant rosemary in a sunny place near the house where it will be handy for your roast lamb and good for picking when in flower. Southernwood makes a superb low hedge or edging, particularly as a framework for rose beds, if it is clipped hard in early spring and then trimmed during the summer to keep it in check.

Many other herbs excel as edging plants – thyme in all its varieties, alpine strawberries, basil, hyssop and parsley. Chives are beautiful when they flower, so plant enough for you to be able to allow this to happen. Chive flowers picked and put into a bottle of white wine vinegar look decorative and flavour the vinegar – you can do the same with the leaves of rosemary and tarragon, and the bottles will look pretty on the kitchen shelf.

Chamomile, thymes, dianthus, and hyssop, all low-growing, will flourish in paving and at the foot of retaining walls. Blue-grey rue contrasts well with dark green leaves, and basil, parsley and golden marjoram all thrive in pots. Mint is always a problem – it is essential for cooking, but should not be allowed to creep into the borders, where it will become an embarrassment. Unless you have the answer in your vegetable garden I advise you to grow it in a container.

Finally, there are the brightly coloured herbs – nasturtiums and marigolds – to illuminate the borders. Consider growing nasturtiums as they do at Giverny, the home of the painter Monet, planting them either side of a wide pathway and allowing them to spread inwards in marvellous shaggy ribbons of green, yellow or orange.

Herbs can be happily incorporated into your borders; conversely, you can incorporate flowers into your herb or vegetable garden. Personally I think that herbs and vegetables make an attractive display on their own account, but there are plenty of annuals and perennials you could include with them. Decide which flowers you use most in your arrangements; if you need more than your borders can give you, or if you would like some to pick but do not want to have them in your borders, this is the place for them. In the herb garden they should complement the textures of the different leaves, but in the vegetable garden they can be allowed to run riot among the carrots and lettuces.

RIBBONS OF NASTURTIUMS *The most colourful of herbs tumbles unrestrained over a wide path in the garden at Giverny of the impressionist painter Claude Monet. Herbs do not have to be solely a green addition to a flower bed. Some have forms with bronze foliage, and many – if allowed to flower – will produce a brilliant display of blooms; borage, hyssop and sage, for example, as well as chives. The starry yellow heads of fennel and dill, however, need to be treated with caution if they are not to spread seeds over the entire garden.*

A Herb Bed
for a Flower Arranger

Herbs do blend well into the flower border, but I have designed a decorative herb corner for the cook who is also a flower arranger with only limited space to spare. Although my selection of plants will do best in the sun – herbs do like sunshine and shelter from the wind – most will provide flavouring and colour even when grown in the shade.

To give additional interest to the design, the central square could be raised, using either timber, such as railway sleepers, or a single brick course. Even a small change in level in the garden immediately adds another element. The four triangular beds are all edged with brick, which helps keep the gravel from straying into them and will emphasize the pattern, especially in winter – herb gardens can look dreary then unless they have a strong design to provide interest when all the herbaceous plants have died back.

The cook will not want for herbs – parsley, thyme, sage, chives, hyssop, fennel, ruby chard, tarragon, basil, rosemary and bay, and nasturtium leaves for the salad. By the side of each entrance, the roses represent a range of colours, but you can make your own choice to reflect the shades you most want. I have tended to select the old-fashioned roses, since they blend best with the herbs. As an alternative, you could clothe a pergola with climbing roses instead of planting Damasks and Bourbons. In summer you will be able to make fragrant posies with the herb leaves, adding touches of colour with the roses or marigolds and nasturtiums.

SUMMER

1 Thyme
2 Ruby Chard
3 Sage (grey)
4 Bronze fennel
5 Parsley
6 *Santolina incana*
7 Rue
8 *Rosa* 'Ispahan'
9 *Rosa* 'Commandant
  Beaurepaire'
10 Chives
11 Lavender 'Hidcote'
12 Hyssop
13 Lovage
14 Winter savory
15 Red orach (*Atriplex
   hortensis* 'Rubra')
16 *Rosa* 'Bredon'
17 Sweet woodruff
18 *Santolina neapolitana*
19 Pennyroyal
20 Coriander
21 Purple sage
22 Fennel
23 *Rosa* 'Tour de Malakoff'
24 *Rosa* 'Magenta'
25 Alpine strawberries
26 Lavender 'Dwarf
   Munstead'
27 *Artemisia absinthium*
   (wormwood)
28 Angelica
29 *Artemisia abrotanum*
   (southernwood)
30 *Rosa* 'Boule de Neige'
31 Basil (pot)
32 Tarragon (pot)
33 Bay or rosemary
34 Nasturtium
35 Marigolds
36 Lilies
37 Scented pelargoniums

FLOWER ARRANGEMENTS THROUGH THE SEASONS

For the flower arranger, some seasons make greater demands upon the garden than others. Each season has its own atmosphere, too, and I urge you to emphasize the differences in your arrangements.

Winter is the time when you will be more in the house than in the garden. Your inclination will probably be for large arrangements of long-lasting berries, leaves and stems; the few precious garden flowers will furnish smaller posies.

Spring starts with an explosion of bulbs; tulips, irises and daffodils offer themselves for more formal arrangements or for great bunches of a single, startling colour. Summer is often full of people and parties. The garden is overflowing, and I am unable to resist filling the house with flowers as well. Autumn is a quieter, more solitary season, an opportunity to be uniquely imaginative about the flowers and foliage you choose.

◆

SPRING FOLIAGE AND FLOWERS

A half-glazed French pot, loosely filled with soft green pittosporum, hellebores and scented 'Cheerfulness', basks in a patch of sun.

SPRING

The slender stems and fresh, pure colours of spring flowers and emerging foliage offer a complete contrast to the boughs and berries of the winter months just past. Suddenly there is a galaxy of brilliant hues from which to select for arrangements – bulbs and primulas first, followed by laden branches of blossom and lilac as spring grows into summer.
Such simple, vivid blooms lend themselves to informal arrangements – jewel posies for a bedside table, careless bunches in bright jugs and single colours massed in a vase.

◆

BUTTER AND CREAM

Leaves of Euonymus radicans edged with gold, complement hyacinths of exactly the same buttery hue. The vase is the focal point of a grouping of modern and antique creamware. Primroses in a small vase set inside a lattice bowl repeat the colour again. Fruit, in this case apricot-coloured Californian plums, can be drawn into an arrangement by a sprinkling of petals.

FLOATING CAMELLIAS

Waxy camellia blooms are always vulnerable to a hard frost which will scorch the petal tips, so, much should be made of perfect blooms. Pale pink camellia heads floating in a low fruit stand set on a silver tray make an elegant dinner-party centrepiece. The dark, polished leaves are often neglected after the flowers are over, but they are almost as beautiful, and can provide a valuable accent for flower arrangements at any time of the year.

PURPLE POSY

A mixture of strong dark colours – claret, violet, mauve and burgundy – is highlighted by splashes of yellow and gold in a posy that should be positioned where the colours can be fully appreciated. The purple glass finger-bowl has a tall, narrow vase inside to give height to this arrangement of pansies, dark red 'Barnhaven' seedling primulas, gold lace primulas, primroses, Euonymus radicans and Clematis macropetala.

SPARKLING TREASURE TROVE

Delicate little spring flowers may not be substantial enough in themselves to be part of a large arrangement, but they can be very impressive if they are grouped together. Jewel-bright primulas contrast with brilliantly coloured old glass. Remember, a small container hidden within the glass will help to support the flowers, but still allows the colour to shine through. The fun of creating a picture like this is choosing each colour as you walk round your garden.

DAINTY DECORATION

Pansies, with their short stems, must be arranged in water as soon as you pick them, before their petals become bruised. They are never sold in florists and can be planted to provide a succession of flowers all through the year. Placed in a frilly little Victorian glass vase, they make a perfect decoration for a dressing table where anything larger might get in the way. The individual beauty of each 'face' will catch your attention as you attend to your own.

SUBTLE SHADES

Catching the late sun is an arrangement in which flowers and foliage are of equal importance and a deliberately restricted spectrum has been used. Fragrant white stems of Osmanthus burkwoodii *and clusters of pachysandra provide white highlights; lime-green* Helleborus corsicus, *yellow* Symphytum grandiflorum, *young foliage of Viburnum farreri and the variegated leaves of Ilex lawsoniana create a background of infinitely various greens and gold. The heavy stoneware vase supports but does not steal the limelight from its contents.*

◆

SPRING BLAZE

It is often a mistake to try to 'arrange' daffodils. They are at their most thrilling as a great sunburst of colour, either a single variety massed together, or, as here, a mixture of different kinds, golden and orange, singles and doubles, large and small trumpets, in a hand-painted jug of equally glorious yellow.

BLUE ON BLUE

Muscari have been chosen to stand next to hyacinths of exactly the same, slightly pink, shade of blue. The natural curve of hyacinth stems is shown to advantage in a spherical vase rather than being forced into a rigid upright stance. The fleshy stems look excellent in glass, but the water must be changed before it clouds. Very simple arrangements suit glass vases better than more complex arrangements – any wire or foam will show and a mixture of stems can look untidy. And, in making such simple arrangements, you have time to observe and become familiar with the special qualities of each spring flower.

◆

BRIDESMAID'S BASKET

In a more sophisticated treatment, lovely little spring flowers – dark pansies, bluebells, forget-me-nots, Clematis montana, viburnum and rosemary among them – have been wired around the edge of a small basket. The centre is filled with cherry blossom to be thrown over the bride and bridegroom as they leave the church.

◆

AN ELEGANT URN

The inherant grace of sprays of Clematis macropetala and C. alpina with silky-centred, delicate violet-blue flowers, has been emphasized as they have been draped down and around a small verdigris urn and pedestal only 1 foot (30 cm) high. The urn has been packed with foam to support the clematis stems.

PALE PINK AND PEWTER
Peony-flowered 'Angelique' tulips –
many-petalled and flushed with pink –
are as easily mistaken for old roses as
they are for peonies. Arranged in a
pewter jug, they are enveloped in a cloud
of white honesty. Tulips age more
beautifully than almost any other flower
as their petals open wider and wider
becoming almost translucent, the single
varieties displaying their central
markings. They continue to look
attractive in a vase until
the petals drop.

RELAXED GRACE

A loose arrangement of flowers often has an artless grace that a more closely packed creation can lack. One burgundy tulip and two vivid pink ones amongst deep-purple lilac, scarcely open, and mauve honesty, have been placed in a wide-necked, softly coloured pot and allowed to fall into position naturally, producing a result that might never be achieved with hours of 'arranging'. The same flowers, joined by branches of blossom, wait for attention (below right), soaking in an old sink, here used as a farmyard water trough.

◆

FLAVOURED WITH SAGE

Pulmonaria are an almost year-round source of white-spotted foliage, but in the spring, they also produce an array of pink flowers turning to blue – 'soldiers and sailors' – which combine well with leaves of purple sage. The delight of these colours is echoed by the texture of the old painted table.

◆

UNITED BY COLOUR

A simple trio of two jugs and a vase in different shades of green (following page) hold flowers and foliage very varied in shape and texture, but unified by their colours – lime green and clear pink. The smallest jug is filled with golden-green sprays of Ribes sanguineum *'Brocklebankii' showing just a few pink flowers. Next to it, pink pelargoniums are mixed with* Helleborus foetidus. *Finally, in the larger green jug, brilliant spikes of* Euphorbia robbiae *are interspersed with electric pink, lily-flowered* Tulipa *'Mariette'.*

SUMMER

As doors and windows are thrown open
wide, making house and garden one,
summer's abundance is reflected in
vases overflowing with colour and
fragrance. This is the ideal opportunity
to create more formal arrangements
around stately spires and full,
impressive flower heads. It is, perhaps,
the only time of the year when you will
be able to achieve an effortless match
between your flowers and the fabric of a
bridesmaid's dress, a favourite
tablecloth or a fall of curtains.
But the richness of summer borders
inspires simple generosity in
arrangements as well as the majestic. A
beautiful shallow dish with individual
blooms floating on the surface is just as
enchanting as the most magnificent
floral centrepiece.

◆

A STUDY IN BLUES

*Flowers in a variety of shades of blue – delphiniums,
beardless irises, Nigella damascena and hardy
geraniums – fill a large, wide-necked bowl. The
diversity of textures is as important as colour; the tall,
spiky flowers create a framework which the feathery ones
fill and soften. The tallest stems at the back give height,
and the arrangement radiates from the centre. The stems
are cut to varying lengths so that there is an impression
of depth. Crumpled wire netting inside the bowl acts as
a support for the flower stems.*

A BRIDE'S BOUQUET

A glorious sheaf of blooms, chiefly pinks and white with touches of soft blue here and there, draws on the wealth of a midsummer border: Astrantia major, saponaria, alstroemeria, scabious, Campanula persicifolia, larkspur, Verbascum phoeniceum, a striped rose and clusters of pale pink roses. Naturally different stem lengths have been used to create the effect of a fall with the bulk of flowers at the top where the bouquet will be held, tapering to a point.

SUMMER PROFUSION

A patterned vase can sometimes create problems by competing with the flowers that it contains, but there is no danger that this delicately striped jug will overwhelm its spectacularly abundant contents among which are peonies and old roses providing necessary weight, sweet peas and sweet williams, foxgloves, stocks, viburnum, honeysuckle, white daisies, euphorbia and, echoing the stripes on the vase, the exquisite pink and carmine clematis 'Nelly Moser'.

PICKED FROM A HERB GARDEN

The kitchen is not the only place for herbs – by themselves or with more conventionally used flowers and foliage, they make exquisite decorations such as the combination of rue, purple sage, artemisia, euonymus and variegated strawberry leaves (above); or rue and purple sage with allium, Alchemilla mollis, bronze fennel and Polygonum bistorta 'Superbum' (right). Both arrangements also include ornamental cabbage – the beautiful leaves come frilly or crinkled, in permutations of blue-grey, pink and cream.

◆

ENCHANTING ROSES

The magic of old roses may be short-lived once they have been cut, but for a few hours there is nothing more ravishing than a bowl replete with Albas and Bourbons, Damasks and Gallicas (following page), heavily scented and with names that capture the imagination like 'Madame Caroline Testout', 'Königen von Dänemark' and 'Fantin Latour'.

DISHES OF PELARGONIUMS

*Two brilliantly coloured shallow dishes,
a round one set inside an oval, are filled
with water. Pelargonium flowers, in
shades of salmon, scarlet and pink, float
on the surface, creating a vivid
centrepiece for a dinner party.
Equally captivating results can be
achieved with other flower heads such as
camellias or clematis.*

POPPIES GALORE

*A huge salmon-pink oriental poppy,
which would not look out of place on a
garden-party hat, is accompanied by
equally sumptuous deep-crimson peonies
and pink and lilac sweet peas (right).
The simplicity of a pot
of scarlet poppies (left) compels you
to notice the rich coal-black
thumb-marks on the paper-like petals,
and the trembling movement of the
myriad stamens.*

TEA IN THE CONSERVATORY

A table set for afternoon tea overflows with a mass of pinks, soft blues and yellows. Tablecloth, china, flowers and even cakes blend in matching shades. A pink jug is filled with blue scabious and Campanula persicifolia, *pink saponaria, larkspur, sweet williams,* Astrantia major *and clusters of small roses, with highlights of lime-green* Alchemilla mollis. *The little cakes on the three-tier cake stand have been decorated with more roses. Creating this scene, for me, is more fun than the tea party afterwards.*

A HARMONIOUS BLEND OF CREAM AND GREEN

*A wide brass bowl lends an exotic Eastern air to an arrangement of green
hydrangeas and Molucella laevis, and cream dahlias and larkspur.*

A TABLESCAPE OF TUSSIE-MUSSIES

*Little posies of flowers, herbs and foliage will make endless pictures. Pick a flower,
carry it round the garden and you are sure to find its natural complement.*

85

An Explosion of Colour

*The colours of late summer are often
vibrant and glowing, exemplified by
dahlias, marigolds, sunflowers and
nasturtiums. Potentially garish, they
need bold handling. Pastel shades will
become insignificant in their company.
Strength of colour is all important.
Unpretentious bright enamel containers,
such as the bucket and jug here, are very
effective. The intensity of colour of these
flowers is such that even combinations of
pink and orange, which might appear to
clash with other kinds of flower, are
vividly successful.*

AUTUMN

The lengthening of shadows as summer draws into autumn does not mean a diminution of colour in the garden. As autumn leaves turn to gold, copper and bronze, berries ripen and the flowers in the border mirror their companion shrubs and trees with an inferno of crimson, ochre, russet and burnt orange. Even the honeyed sunlight conspires to fan this last blaze of colour.

This is a time to create a personal style in your arrangements. The supply of material is more disparate than at any other time of the year, with blooms large and small, seed heads, foliage, berries, stems and branches in all shapes and sizes from which to choose.

◆

HARVEST FESTIVAL

An informal arrangement of flowers, berries, fruit, seed heads and grasses marks the transition from late summer into autumn. The vivid sun colours of the flowers are complemented by the choice of brilliant turquoise-blue vases and bowls. Fennel heads, grasses and Molucella laevis soften the colouring.

BOUNTIFUL BERRIES

An assortment of pyracantha berries, from yellow through orange and red, crab apples, rose hips and autumn foliage in a plain white jug makes an impressive, richly coloured display.

◆

AUTUMNAL ASYMMETRY

Broad, fleshy bergenia leaves taking on rich, autumnal tints are an unusual touch in an asymmetrical arrangement with roses and pink sorbus berries, created in a shallow, wood container.

A BASKET OF HYDRANGEAS

The mop heads of Hydrangea macrophylla are almost more beautiful once they have started to mellow than when they are in their vivid prime. The subtle colouring of the individual florets becomes more apparent. The heads can easily be dried by standing them in a jar in a few inches of water and leaving them until the water has all evaporated. They can then grace arrangements through the winter months.

WINTER

Short days and long nights mean that winter vases are often lit by electric lamps or candles which subtly alter the colours they illuminate. Sometimes it is easier to wait until after dark to create winter arrangements. Berries, stems and leaves form their substance, with dried flowers recalling the warmth of summer. Winter is also the time when you will be most aware of the patterns and shapes in the garden, with snow and frost whitening the ground. This may be reflected in the coloured or twisted stems you bring inside. These 'see-through' arrangements can make striking patterns on a background wall.

◆

EVERLASTING BEAUTY

Dried flowers, delicately coloured like fading antique silks and brocades are arranged in a low dome that can be viewed from all sides on a dining table. All the flowers – roses, camellias, alliums, eryngium, helichrysum and honesty – are easily dried at home.

PRECIOUS BLOOMS

Winter flowers should be treasured; there will never be enough for a large arrangement but they are all the more valuable for their scarcity. Display them in small vases – singly or just a few blooms in each. Here, Christmas roses, snowdrops, a white hyacinth and sprigs of silver and variegated foliage are carried in the glasses of a specimen stand which has been set in a window where they will be illuminated by the rays of winter sunshine. The scale of the flowers is revealed when they are compared with a vase of forced hyacinths and white and green variegated leaves (below far left.)

◆

A BOWL OF GOSSAMER

Clematis seed heads, so fine that they will blow away in the slightest breeze, look lovely in a frosted glass dish (below left). They will last longer indoors if they are lightly fixed with hair spray.

◆

WINTER ENCHANTMENT

Reflecting the frost and snow outside, an arrangement of decorative, drooping Garrya elliptica catkins, silver honesty 'pennies', contorted hazel and clematis seed heads shimmers in the winter light. Christmas roses, discovered nestling in the light sprinkling of snow outside, contrast in their delicacy with the wiry toughness of the garrya and hazel.

POT-POURRI BASKET

Fragrant pot-pourri filling a roughly woven basket is surrounded by dried flowers – claret-red peonies, roses, seed heads of Nigella damascena and honesty, eryngium and blue larkspur – wired around the basket rim. Shells echo the rich colours, and generous sheaves of honesty, eryngium and poppy seed heads lie in the background.

LAVENDER BLUE

Baskets of lavender spikes stand in front of a wreath of dried flowers and seed heads in shades of grey, blue, lavender, cream and soft green. Although dried flowers are now increasingly easy to buy, it is worth drying your own so that you have a supply of your garden flowers – like the scabious in this wreath – to use.

DECORATIVE WREATH

*Red apples, walnuts and starry
Viburnum tinus flowers, tied into a
wreath of conifer foliage, hang on the
front door, welcoming visitors who have
braved the cold weather (left and near
right). Use plenty of foliage when
making a wreath, otherwise it may look a
little ungenerous.*

◆

FRESH GARLANDS

*Swags of ivy – plain and variegated –
make a fresh alternative to paper and
tinsel decorations and recall winter
festivities of a previous age. They are not
difficult to make: the lengths of ivy are
simply wired on to rope. Anemones
and fern fronds next to a bowl of
kumquats are another fresh touch.*

◆

TWO POSIES FOR COLD WEATHER

*Winter jasmine, Christmas roses,
snowdrops and Helleborus foetidus
with gold-and-green variegated
euonymus and holly radiate colour and
freshness from a low blue bowl filled
with moss (centre right) – proof that
winter is not just a season of neutral
shades. Another low bowl seen from
above (far right) contains a ring of
silver-flecked leaves of Cyclamen
hederifolium with a small bunch of
purple Helleborus orientalis
peeping out of the centre.*

ESSENTIAL PLANTS
FOR THE FLOWER
ARRANGER'S GARDEN

*It is not easy to select only sixty-four plants
to form the backbone of a flower arranger's
garden. My original list, plants chosen at
random, became much too long, so I have
had to decide firmly on priorities.*

*Winter is the leanest time, so I have
included at least twenty-five plants whose
leaves, flowers, coloured stems, seed heads
or dried flowers will be useful during these
months. There are broad-leaved evergreens,
dogwood, willows and nut for interesting
stems. There should never be a moment
when you are without flowers to pick. The
stragglers from autumn, like violas and
roses, usually carry on until the true winter
flowers open – snowdrops, hellebores, winter
aconites, Jasminum nudiflorum and the
first willow catkins. Leaves of holly,
eucalyptus, bergenia, euonymus, ferns and
many ivies can be used as background and
sometimes as the main theme in your
arrangements, which can also include dried
flowers and fruits, physalis or Chinese
lanterns, and honesty pennies.*

◆

ESSENTIAL FOLIAGE
*Broad, stately and never to be found in a florist, hostas are an
invaluable source of impressive leaves and flowers that will
lend scale to arrangements.*

My next consideration was herbaceous plants and low shrubs with beautiful leaves which will be useful through spring until autumn, such as hostas, more ferns, santolina, rosemary, *Alchemilla mollis*. Flowers for the same months must be long-lasting, sweetly scented or repeat-flowering such as dahlias, or, like clematis, flowers you will never find in the florist. Roses are essential, and each gardener should choose his or her own favourites. I have left out the flowers which are cheap to buy – spring anemones, gladioli and chrysanthemums – but would love to have included poppies for their spectacular and fleeting beauty. My selection may be quite different from yours, but it will form a basis for your own ideas.

KEY TO PLANT HARDINESS

The degree of cold that each plant included in this selection can survive has been given, but it is important to remember that these gradings of hardiness are only approximate – protection during the winter months, shelter or well-drained soil, for example, can cause the plant to survive much lower temperatures.

EXTREMELY HARDY Generally hardy to temperatures below − 29° C (− 20° F), in some cases can survive temperatures as low as − 40° C (− 40° F).

VERY HARDY Generally hardy to − 18° C (0° F), in some cases can survive temperatures as low as − 29° C (− 20° F).

MODERATELY TO VERY HARDY Hardy to about − 15° to − 18° C (5−0° F).

MODERATELY HARDY Hardy to below − 6° C (21° F), in many cases hardy to below − 12° to − 15° C (10−5° F).

SEMI-HARDY Able to withstand frosts to − 6° C (21° F) at most, in many cases less.

TENDER Not hardy below − 1° C (30° F), needs protection from frost.

PHILADELPHUS
Mock orange

Deciduous shrubs
White flowers

Moderately to very hardy
SIZE 3–10ft (90cm–3m)
ASPECT Prefers sun, tolerates light shade
SOIL Good, well drained
GOOD ASSOCIATES Spring bulbs, expecially snowdrops, other white-flowered shrubs, such as *Spiraea × arguta*

USE *Flowers in summer. Ideally, the leaves should be stripped from the stems.*

The mock oranges, with their beautiful, richly scented white flowers, are some of the most delightful shrubs in the garden, and stems of the flowers are lovely in summer flower arrangements. My favourite small shrub is *Philadelphus microphyllus*, which is small enough to be used at the front of a shrub or mixed border. Slightly taller is the delightfully fragrant P. 'Belle Étoile' (above): its flowers have a maroon central blotch. P. 'Sybille' has rather arching branches and an orange scent. For a philadelphus to use as a tall shrub at the back of the border I would choose P. *coronarius*, P. 'Beauclerk' or P. 'Burfordensis'.

To encourage new growth, remove one-third of the oldest flowering wood each year, after flowering. Philadelphus benefit from firm pruning. I have a P. *coronarius* which to my knowledge has been in this garden for fifty years and which through hard pruning is still in very good heart. I associate its blossom with Midsummer's Day.

CHRYSANTHEMUM MAXIMUM
Shasta daisy

Herbaceous perennials
White flowers

Moderately to very hardy
SIZE 2–4ft (60–120cm)
ASPECT Full sun in temperate climates; in hot climates, light shade
SOIL Rich, moist, well drained
GOOD ASSOCIATES Spring bulbs, dicentra, *Centaurea montana*, *Malva moschata*, penstemon, *Salvia turkestanica*, *Sedum* 'Autumn Joy', *S. spectabile*

USE *Flowers from midsummer to autumn. The quality of the flowers will be better if you divide the clumps frequently.*

Hardy chrysanthemums are indispensable in the border and for cutting. They are easy to cultivate and flower freely over a considerable period. Use them as mid-border plants, with earlier herbaceous plants, such as *Centaurea montana*, in front and nearby.

I recommend 'Snowcap' (below), a single with a bright yellow eye; 'Alaska', an old single with a yellow eye; 'Wirral Pride' and 'Esther Read', both double; and 'Aglaia', a double with very quilled petals, and a hint of yellow in its centre. All these are white. I also grow the pink-flowered *Chrysanthemum rubellum* 'Clara Curtis', which flowers from late summer till frost, and lasts as long as four weeks in water.

All these chrysanthemums work hard for you, so keep them well fed, with an autumn mulching and bonemeal in spring. Divide them every other year, preferably in spring.

SALIX
Willow

Deciduous trees and shrubs
Red or yellow stems; yellow to grey
and pink catkins

Extremely hardy
SIZE From ground cover to large tree
ASPECT Most do best in full sun
SOIL Moist
GOOD ASSOCIATES Spring-flowering shrubs
such as hamamelis, chimonanthus;
snowdrops or crocus for underplanting

USE *Stems in winter, catkins in spring*

Two willows which are particularly attractive for their coloured winter stems are *Salix alba* 'Chermesina', with scarlet stems, and golden-stemmed *S. alba* 'Vitellina'. A selection of these stems in moss in a shallow vase makes a simple but beautiful display. These two willows should be pollarded in early spring to give them time to grow their coloured wands for winter.

Many willows have exciting catkins. *S. sachalinensis* 'Sekka' is much prized by flower arrangers for its silver catkins borne on wide, flat stems. The interesting black catkins of *S.* 'Melanostachys' are useful in many arrangements. I particularly like *S.* 'Eugenei', with lovely small pink catkins, and another favourite is *S. daphnoides* 'Aglaia', which has catkins in midwinter. The purple shoots of this willow have a white bloom, and the catkins are silvery with a purple sheen, until the yellow pollen ripens. *S.* 'Wehrhahnii' (above) has snow-white male catkins up to 1½in (4cm) long.

GALANTHUS
Snowdrop

Bulbs
White flowers

Very hardy
SIZE 3–8in (7.5–20cm)
ASPECT Sunny in winter, with shade from
trees and shrubs in summer
SOIL Rich, well drained, does best of
all in chalky soil
GOOD ASSOCIATES Winter aconites,
evergreen ground cover such
as ivy, waldsteinia

USE *Flowers in winter. They last*
well in water.

Nothing is more exciting in the garden in winter than a great carpet of snowdrops, increased over the years. And by cultivating a range of species, it is possible to have snowdrops in flower from autumn until spring. *Galanthus nivalis* subsp. *reginae-olgae*, for instance, always causes amazement by flowering before the leaves appear in autumn. Start with the common snowdrop, *G. nivalis*, but all the species are easy to cultivate, extremely hardy, and suitable to grow in rough-mown grass. If you have a few near you in a small vase, you will be able to enjoy the subtle differences which occur in the species.

Snowdrops like a spell of cold, and dislike being baked in summer. Plant them 2in (5cm) deep, in grass, in the border, under deciduous shrubs or through evergreen ground cover. To increase your stock, divide and replant immediately after flowering.

ZANTEDESCHIA AETHIOPICA
Arum lily

Rhizomatous perennials
White or green flowers

Moderately hardy
SIZE 3–4¼ft (90–130cm)
ASPECT Full sun
SOIL Rich, very moist
GOOD ASSOCIATES Dark climbers such as
Vitis vinifera 'Purpurea'

USE *Flowers from mid- to late summer*

The best-known form of arum lily is *Zantedeschia aethiopica* 'Crowborough' (above), with its huge pure white flowers and glossy green spear-shaped foliage. Even more exotic is *Z. aethiopica* 'Green Goddess', which has a large green flower with a white throat. Both are striking in arrangements.

In the garden, they look their loveliest, and do best, in or near water – they thrive planted in mud in deep water, below the line where the water becomes frozen. If you don't have a pond, prepare a rich soil and plant the young roots 4in (10cm) deep. To protect the crowns from frost, cover them with a heavy mulch in winter. In a temperate climate it takes arum lilies two or three years to become established, and after that they will begin slowly to increase. In hot, humid conditions, such as they find in parts of north-eastern Australia, they spread so fast they will take over an area unless they are kept in check.

GYPSOPHILA PANICULATA
Baby's breath

Herbaceous perennials
White or pink flowers

Moderately hardy
SIZE 3–4ft (90–120cm)
ASPECT Full sun
SOIL Alkaline, well cultivated, well drained
GOOD ASSOCIATES *Acanthus spinosus*, late
spring bulbs

USE *Flowers from midsummer to autumn*

Gypsophila is seen more often as a cut flower
in the florist than in the garden: perhaps its
slow initial development and dislike of being
moved make people reluctant to grow it. But
do persevere – the impact of the mass of tiny
flowers is as light and airy in the border as it
is in your flower arrangements. In both, the
feathery panicles of starry flowers on wiry
stems give an overall effect of an attractive
veil draped over the grey-green leaves.

The most easily obtained gypsophilas are
Gypsophila paniculata 'Rosy Veil', with
semi-double pink flowers, and G. *paniculata*
'Bristol Fairy' (above), with double white
flowers on 3ft (90cm) stems.

Gypsophila should be planted in spring.
The long tap roots hate to be disturbed, so
either get young container-grown plants or
sow seed in the flowering position and wait
patiently. A full-grown plant is well worth
waiting for.

STACHYS LANATA
Lamb's tongue, lamb's ears

Evergreen perennials
Inconspicuous pink flowers; white-grey
leaves

Extremely hardy
SIZE 20in (50cm)
ASPECT Full sun
SOIL Any soil will do, even a very
poor, dry one
GOOD ASSOCIATES Spring bulbs, other grey
foliage plants, evergreens, pink, blue and
mauve flowers

USE *Young leaves in summer, dried*
flower stems later

Stachys make marvellous carpeting plants in
the garden, and background plants in arrangements. They also have the virtue of
being very easy to acquire – you will certainly have a friend who is only too pleased
to give you some.

I like them at the corners of my borders
and in bold drifts in proportion to the
border size. Early spring bulbs such as
chionodoxas, crocus and *Iris reticulata* can
be planted through them, as can the slightly
later Dutch iris and *Gladiolus × colvillei*. For
nearby choose other grey foliage plants, such
as santolinas, or dark evergreens, pink
diascias or blue veronicas, *Heuchera* 'Palace
Purple' or *Sedum* 'Autumn Joy'.

When the flowers start to fade in summer,
cut the flower stems, bunch them, and hang
them upside down in a cool place to dry, for
your winter arrangements. Remove any dead
leaves at the same time as the flowers.

LUNARIA
Honesty

Annuals, biennials or herbaceous
perennials
White or pale-mauve to wine-red and
deep-purple flowers

Extremely hardy
SIZE 2¼ft (70cm)
ASPECT Any
SOIL Rich, with leaf mould
GOOD ASSOCIATES *Kerria japonica*,
forsythia, Loddon lilies, white or bright
red tulips, *Galtonia candicans*

USE *Flowers in spring, silvery discs of*
seed heads throughout the year

To make the most of the silver 'pennies' at
the heart of honesty seed heads (above),
remove the outer cases of the seed heads to
reveal their shiny surfaces, give them a dark
green background and place the vase where
the winter sun can shine through the silver.

The common form of honesty, *Lunaria
annua*, has violet-lilac flowers, but you can
get forms with white and deep-red to rich-
purple flowers. The form, *L. annua* 'Alba',
with white flowers, has white-marked leaves.
In the light of a spring evening this white
honesty looks beautifully ghost-like. Plant
them with bright red tulips.

L. annua is best treated as a biennial. *L.
rediviva*, with fragrant purple flowers and
oval seed heads, is a perennial.

Honesty roots do not transplant well,
except when very young. Collect your own
seeds and sow them in spring. Plant them in
groups for maximum effect.

SANTOLINA
Cotton lavender

Evergreen shrubs
Grey leaves

Semi-hardy
SIZE 20in (50cm)
ASPECT Full sun
SOIL Well drained
GOOD ASSOCIATES Pink, mauve
and blue flowers

USE *Leaf sprays throughout the year,*
especially in winter. They last well in
water.

Santolina, with its aromatic grey leaves, is an
indispensable plant in the border, and extremely useful as a back-up in vases. The two
best varieties are *Santolina incana*, with
thread-like silvery foliage, and *S. neapolitana*
(above), which is similar but with more
feathery leaves and a laxer habit of growth.
Use them as lovely mounds of grey in a
border – they look well emphasizing a corner. *S. incana* can also be grown as a low
hedge, or serve to line a pathway.

If you clip your santolina hard back to the
old wood each spring it will remain a shapely
bush for years, and you will be saved the
embarrassment of its harsh yellow flowers.
It roots easily from stems clipped off during
pruning. Do wait until spring to prune,
though – the old growth acts as a frost
protection during the winter.

NARCISSUS
Daffodil

Bulbs
Flowers in white, cream, and every shade
of yellow, often with pink to orange
trumpets

Moderately to very hardy
SIZE 3–20in (8–50cm)
ASPECT Sun or light shade
SOIL Any soil will do
GOOD ASSOCIATES Spring-flowering shrubs,
early tulips, wallflowers, forget-me-nots

USE *Flowers in spring*

Daffodils, naturalized in drifts in grass, or in
the border, are one of the joys of the spring
garden. There is a huge range of different
varieties available. Study the autumn bulb
catalogues carefully, and choose the colours
and heights you want. If you spread the
flowering time, you will be able to have
daffodils in flower throughout the spring.
Some are more scented than others – usually
the medium- and small-cupped types. I am
particularly fond of the small, fragrant
jonquilla daffodils, especially *Narcissus*
'Trevithian' and *N.* 'Baby Moon'. Among
the large-cupped types, one of my favourites
is *N.* 'Ice Follies' (below).

Plant the bulbs at the depth recommended
for the particular variety: most need to be
quite deep. For naturalizing they should be
12in (30cm) apart, to allow for spreading.
Miniatures should be 4–6in (10–15cm)
apart. If you have them in the border, lifting
them when they fade to make space for
summer flowers, they can be closer together.

OSMANTHUS DELAVAYI

Evergreen shrubs
White flowers; green leaves

Moderately hardy
SIZE 5ft (150cm) after 5 years, ultimate
height 7ft (2m)
ASPECT Full sun to medium shade
SOIL Well drained
GOOD ASSOCIATES Daffodils, tulips,
summer-flowering herbaceous plants

USE *Flowers in spring, leaves throughout*
the year

Osmanthus delavayi is one of my favourite
evergreen shrubs. It has small, neat leaves
and jasmine-like white flowers. Both leaves
and flowers have a delicious scent, which in
the garden 'wafts upon the air'.

This osmanthus makes an excellent specimen or background shrub. In my garden it is
growing in a windy corner and has never
been seriously set back in winter, though the
leaves were once scorched by early spring
winds. It is very fast-growing, putting on at
least 12in (30cm) of growth each year, but
can be kept in control by pruning and
clipping. There is the great advantage that
the tell-tale gaps where you have cut its
branches for spring arrangements will soon
be hidden with new growth.

O. heterophyllus is a good evergreen with
white scented flowers which appear in the
autumn. If you would like variegated leaves,
try *O. heterophyllus* 'Variegatus'. Both will
pick well for your arrangements.

VIBURNUM

Deciduous shrubs
White or pink flowers; red berries

Very hardy
SIZE 3–7ft (1–2m)
ASPECT Most prefer light shade
SOIL Any soil will do
GOOD ASSOCIATES Spring bulbs; autumn-
flowering clematis to grow through

USE *Flowers in winter or spring, berries*
in autumn

The deciduous viburnums make good medium to large shrubs. Their winter or spring flowers, which are often fragrant, are lovely in arrangements, and they also fruit well, with red, or occasionally yellow, berries. I particularly like the translucent yellow berries of *Viburnum opulus* 'Fructuluteo', which look very dramatic in arrangements.

For winter flowers I would choose *V. × bodnantense*, with large, very fragrant blooms, pink opening to white. This bush has an upright habit, so it will not sprawl over its neighbours, and consequently can be used in a mixed border. Of the spring-flowering scented viburnums, the standard *V. × carlcephalum* and *V. × burkwoodii* are particularly good. I am fond of *V. opulus* 'Sterile', the snowball bush, whose white flowers appear in late spring. However, it needs stern pruning to keep it to its allotted space. I also recommend *V. plicatum* 'Mariesii' (above) and *V. plicatum* 'Lanarth', two striking and shapely shrubs, with branches growing in horizontal tiers.

In general, the deciduous species require only shaping and removal of dead wood.

CORYLUS AVELLANA 'CONTORTA'
Twisted nut, Harry Lauder's walking stick

Deciduous shrubs
Yellow-green catkins

Moderately to very hardy; will tolerate winds, and frost up to 20°F (−6°C)
SIZE 10ft (3m) after 25 years
ASPECT Full sun to deepest shade
SOIL Any soil will do
GOOD ASSOCIATES Spring bulbs,
erythronium, hellebores, cowslips

USE *Catkins and twisted stems in winter*
and early spring

The twisted stems of *Corylus avellana* 'Contorta' make a useful standby for winter and early spring decoration. The stems can be used on their own or with spring bulbs. I gave two stems to a friend one December, and she still had them the next winter, ready to use again when flowers are scarce.

Try to give this corylus an open site where its shape can be seen to advantage – if it is crowded in among bulky shrubs, its individual twisty character will be hidden; so too will the yellowish-green catkins which develop in late winter.

No pruning is necessary, but when you cut stems for decoration it is best to take them from ground level, to encourage new growth from the base.

As an alternative to this corylus, you could grow the Pekin willow, *Salix matsudana* 'Tortuosa', which also has twisted branches.

ANTHEMIS TINCTORIA
Golden marguerite

Herbaceous perennials
Yellow flowers

Extremely hardy
SIZE 2½–3ft (75–100cm)
ASPECT Full sun
SOIL Well drained, not too fertile (in rich
soil they will grow
leggy and flower less frequently)
GOOD ASSOCIATES *Alchemilla mollis*, golden-
leaved or golden-marked hostas, *Iris pallida* 'Aureo-variegata', blue flowers such as *Campanula persicifolia* and willow gentian, white flowers such as nicotiana

USE *Flowers from early summer to late*
autumn. They last well in water.

Anthemis tinctoria flowers for weeks on end, starting at the very beginning of summer and continuing right through until the first frosts. *A. tinctoria* 'E.C. Buxton' (above) is a good variety, both for garden value and for picking. It forms a neat mound of fern-like leaves and carries its pale yellow daisy flowers on strong stems. It is admirable as a cut flower, and the plant itself benefits if flowers are removed frequently.

A. tinctoria is a front-of-the-border flower, particularly effective in front of border phlox or other plants which get untidy round their bases as the summer moves on. Cut down the flower stems as they fade, to encourage new flowers. If the centre of the clump looks bare in spring, divide it and use sections of the healthy outside growth to form new clumps.

LIGUSTRUM OVALIFOLIUM 'ARGENTEUM' and 'AUREUM'
Privet

Evergreen or deciduous shrubs
Green leaves marked with silver or gold

Very hardy
SIZE 10ft (3m) after 5 years, ultimate
height 20ft (6m)
ASPECT Needs sun to retain variegation
SOIL Rich, but will grow in less good
conditions if fed
GOOD ASSOCIATES Spring or autumn-
flowering clematis, to grow through

USE *Leaves throughout the year. The*
stems will stay fresh in water for weeks,
sometimes even forming roots.

Either of these variegated privets can be used
to provide a strong element in a mixed
border, or placed at a distance from the
house to form a focal point. They are also
extremely useful to the flower arranger. The
small leaves are easy to use indoors, and their
colour shines up well in artificial light. The
leaves of *Ligustrum ovalifolium* 'Argenteum'
are grey-green with soft creamy-white edges,
those of *L. ovalifolium* 'Aureum' (above), the
golden privet, glow yellow with green centres. Privet flowers are very strongly scented
so use them sparingly indoors.

Privet is a greedy shrub: feed it well with a
general fertilizer. It clips well, and an annual
trim, or the natural pruning that will occur if
you use the young growth for picking, will
help it to keep its lower growth. If your
shrub has outgrown its allotted space you
can cut it back hard, even to ground level.

LONICERA NITIDA 'BAGGESEN'S GOLD'

Evergreen shrubs
Golden leaves

Very hardy
SIZE 3ft (90cm) after 5 years, ultimate
height 5ft (150cm)
ASPECT Needs full sun to keep its
golden leaves
SOIL Any soil will do, so long as it is
neither excessively dry nor too damp
GOOD ASSOCIATES Bergenias, other golden
plants, such as *Lonicera japonica*
'Aureo-reticulata', or plants with blue
flowers to contrast

USE *Leaves throughout the year*

The golden-leaved form of the common
Lonicera nitida is a most useful shrub for
picking. The stems are stiff when older, but
the new growth hangs gracefully. The leaves
are small – only $\frac{1}{8}$–$\frac{1}{4}$in (5–10mm) long – so
make good backing for arrangements of
small spring bulbs; in winter they associate
well with Christmas roses and sprigs of *L.*
fragrantissima.

L. nitida is very fast-growing, and the more
you cut it the firmer the shrub becomes – in
fact it needs clipping to prevent it becoming
leggy. I grow several in containers as small
standards with mop heads. I have also seen it
used as a dwarf hedging plant, clipped se-
verely twice a year to keep it in proper trim.

Like all loniceras, this shrub roots easily
from soft or hardwood cuttings. It will
transplant easily even when it has grown as
large as 3ft (90cm).

JASMINUM NUDIFLORUM
Winter jasmine

Deciduous climbing shrubs
Yellow flowers

Moderately to very hardy
SIZE 7ft (2m)
ASPECT Sun or shade
SOIL Any soil will do, even a poor one
GOOD ASSOCIATES *Clematis viticella*
to grow through

USE *Flowers throughout the winter*

The winter-flowering jasmine is one of the
best standbys for the flower arranger during
the dead season. It is reliable, easy to pick,
and with adequate wall or other support will
grow in any odd corner where most other
shrubs languish. I have also seen it grown as a
pyramid trained on a frame, and showing off
its winter flowers and glossy summer foliage
as a central feature in a mixed border.

Jasmine's greatest attraction, though, lies
in the way in which the yellow flower buds,
with their gentle hint of red on the reverse of
each petal, will open, one after the other,
along the green stems when brought indoors.
In arrangements it mixes well with dark-
green evergreen leaves, with the first
snowdrops, with Christmas roses and with
red berries.

Prune winter jasmine just after it has
flowered – this is important, as it flowers on
new wood.

ERANTHIS HYEMALIS
Winter aconite

Herbaceous perennials with tuberous roots
Yellow flowers

Moderately to very hardy
SIZE 2–4in (5–10cm)
ASPECT Sunny in winter, with shade from trees and shrubs in summer
SOIL Alkaline, but will tolerate acid
GOOD ASSOCIATES Plant under deciduous trees or shrubs, such as witch hazel or *Viburnum farreri*, with crocus, scillas and other spring bulbs

USE *Flowers in late winter*

Winter aconites are among the first of the small flowers to appear in late winter. They will even push their way through the snow, and when the ground is frozen they will just be waiting for a thaw. They are a cheering sight in a shallow moss-filled dish. I also like to dig up a few plants just as they appear through the soil and plant them in a dish, so that I can watch them develop indoors.

You will be able to collect seed in mid-spring. The leaves disappear soon after this, so aconites are not a good subject for a border, where they may be forked in by mistake. You could try putting a small clump into the rock garden, sowing on top a crop of small annuals such as eschscholzias, mesembryanthemums or dwarf nasturtiums. But the best place for them is definitely under deciduous trees or shrubs, where the ground is shaded by foliage during the summer months.

RUDBECKIA
Coneflower

Herbaceous perennials and hardy annuals
Flowers in shades from golden to a rich bronze-red

Extremely hardy
SIZE 3ft (90cm)
ASPECT Prefers sun
SOIL Any good garden soil
GOOD ASSOCIATES Almost any autumn flowers; can replace lupins or sweet williams after they have flowered

USE *Flowers from midsummer until frost*

It was the dress designer Hardy Amies who taught me how extremely useful the annual rudbeckia is for massing in a vase to spectacular effect. It has taken me many years to realize how effective annuals can be. They flower more profusely than perennials and often have more vivid colours. And you can try new things each year.

One of my favourite annual rudbeckias is *Rudbeckia* 'Marmalade' (below), whose name admirably describes its rich red-gold colour. If you sow the seeds in trays in mid- to late spring, the plants should be ready to put out at midsummer, to fill any gaps in the borders.

Of the perennial rudbeckias I do like *R.* 'Goldsturm', a black-eyed susan about 3ft (90cm) high, and also the rudbeckias that are now classed as *Echinacea purpurea*, which are a most alluring crimson-purple and will make good clumps in two years. The finest of these is *E. purpurea* 'Bressingham Hybrid'.

FORSYTHIA × INTERMEDIA 'SPECTABILIS'
Golden bell bush

Deciduous shrubs
Yellow flowers

Moderately to very hardy
SIZE 8ft (2.5m)
ASPECT Prefers full sun, but will tolerate light shade
SOIL Fertile
GOOD ASSOCIATES *Elaeagnus pungens* 'Maculata', spring bulbs, primroses

USE *Branches of opening buds in early spring*

Forsythia opens its flowers in early spring, showing off their bright yellow petals, spectacular but scentless, along the length of the stem. It is very accommodating: it does equally well trained against a wall, as a free-standing shrub – if there is space, a group of three looks lovely – or as one of the shrubs in a mixed hedge.

Forsythia is quick and easy to establish, flowering on young wood. One-third of the flowering wood should be cut back each year after flowering, to encourage new growth. An old neglected bush can be rejuvenated by hard pruning, taking all except the young wood to ground level. It will then flower again in two years' time. Take cuttings of semi-ripe wood in summer, or hardwood cuttings in winter.

PHYSALIS ALKEKENGI FRANCHETII

Chinese lantern, Cape gooseberry, winter cherry, bladder cherry

Herbaceous perennials
Orange or blood-red seed pods

Moderately to very hardy
SIZE 2ft (60cm)
ASPECT Sun or shade
SOIL Any soil will do
GOOD ASSOCIATES *Iris foetidissima*, honesty

USE *Seed pods in winter. The pods can be used while they are still green, as well as after they have turned orange or red.*

Physalis are lovely in winter, when their seed pods have turned to orange, but during the summer they are rather untidy plants, and their strawberry-like flowers are inconspicuous, so it is best to site them behind deciduous plants or shrubs, where they will be hidden in summer, but their bright lanterns will show up later. The seed pods will last for weeks outside; picked and used indoors they will keep their lustre all through the winter.

For an interesting winter effect, try grouping some physalis with *Iris foetidissima* – whose orange seeds will match the Chinese lanterns – and a backing of shining silver honesty 'pennies'.

Grown from seed, physalis will start to flower the second year. They may be increased by division in spring.

ALSTROEMERIA
Peruvian Lily

Herbaceous perennials
Pink, red, orange or yellow flowers

Moderately to very hardy
SIZE 3–4ft (90–120cm)
ASPECT Sunny
SOIL Fertile, well drained
GOOD ASSOCIATES Perovskia, *Anaphalis triplinervis*, dwarf delphiniums, *Artemisia* 'Powis Castle' and A. 'Silver Queen'.

USE *Flowers in summer. They last well in water.*

Alstroemerias are beautifully marked, lily-like flowers, their large heads carried on wiry stems, their narrow leaves limp. *Alstroemeria ligtu* and its hybrids, which vary in colour from reddish-pink to blush, make a good choice for the small garden. *A. aurantiaca* (below), which comes in strong orange or bright yellow, is more invasive, and so better suited for the larger garden.

The best way to establish alstroemerias is to follow G.S. Thomas's advice: plant pot-grown specimens 10in (25cm) deep in late summer when they are dormant, marking the spot; their first winter give them a thick mulch to protect them against frost damage; increase your stock by sowing seed directly into the border as soon as it is ripe in autumn. You can buy seed, but make sure that it is fresh.

If you want to move alstroemerias, dig out square pieces without disturbing or removing the soil around the roots, which are very easily damaged.

PYRACANTHA
Firethorn

Evergreen shrubs
Red and yellow berries

Very hardy; if top growth is killed by frost, it will regenerate from bottom growth
SIZE 7ft (2m) after 5 years, ultimate height 14ft (4m)
ASPECT Shade
SOIL Any except the extremely alkaline

USE *Berries in late winter*

The bright berries of the firethorn make a spectacular effect in the garden on dark winter days. Pyracantha can be grown either on a wall or as a free-standing shrub. I like it against a wall, tied in firmly but with some arching branches allowed to cascade out. It is a source of joy, planted on the wall of your house where it can encroach on a window, and where the evening sun will shine on and through its branches. My choice for a house wall would be *Pyracantha atalantioides* (for scarlet berries), *P. rogersiana* (orange berries, above), or *P. rogersiana* 'Flava' (yellow berries). *P.* 'Mohave' has a more spreading habit, so is more suitable for a garden wall.

Prune pyracantha lightly, remembering that it flowers, and therefore fruits, on both old and new wood. For some reason, the birds leave pyracantha berries alone.

AQUILEGIA
Columbine, granny's bonnet

Herbaceous perennials
Flowers of many colours

Very hardy
SIZE 1–3ft (30–90cm)
ASPECT Sun or light shade
SOIL Any good garden soil
GOOD ASSOCIATES Iris, lupins, poppies

USE *Flowers in spring and early summer*

Aquilegias are definitely among my top ten plants, for the garden and for cutting. The foliage is beautiful, and the flowers, proudly carried on strong, wiry stems, a boon to flower arrangers.

As a selection of aquilegias, I would recommend particularly *Aquilegia vulgaris*, the common granny's bonnet, our native wild flower with deep blue colouring and short spurs, A. 'McKana Giant Hybrids', which carries large flowers and long spurs in a huge colour range, and A. 'Nora Barlow', an unusual variety with no spurs and double pink and green flowers. A. 'Olympia Red and Gold' (above) is another of the hybrids of *A. vulgaris*.

Plant aquilegias in profusion in the shady part of the garden, and add a few at the front of the border, where they will be seen to their full advantage. If you allow some to set and disperse their seeds, you will have a new generation.

BERGENIA
Elephant's ears

Evergreen perennials
White, pink or red flowers; leaves green,
often with a reddish tinge in winter

Very hardy
SIZE 1–2ft (30–60cm)
ASPECT Sun or shade; the best winter leaf colour comes with a sunny position
SOIL Not too rich
GOOD ASSOCIATES Plants with strap-like leaves, such as yuccas and *Phormium tenax*

USE *Leaves all the year round, flowers in late winter and spring. The leaves last well in water.*

Bergenias are very versatile. Ideal for ground cover, for awkward sites and for creating bold effects by steps and gateways, they will thrive in such notoriously difficult conditions as dry shade, clay soils and seaside gardens. They provide the flower arranger with flowers for cutting and, above all, with handsome winter foliage. However, both leaves and flowers may be damaged by frost.

The hardiest and most common bergenia is *Bergenia cordifolia* (below), with deep pink flowers. *B. cordifolia* 'Purpurea' is taller and has magenta flowers and leaves which colour well. Among the hybrids, B. 'Ballawley' has crimson flowers, red leaves and flower stems, and warrants shelter. There are some fine Bressingham hybrids, including B. 'Bressingham White'.

Bergenias are easy to increase: just break off old fleshy stems in winter and bury them deeply. They will then form new roots.

CORNUS ALBA
Red-barked dogwood

Deciduous shrubs
Red or yellow stems

Very hardy
SIZE 7ft (2m)
ASPECT Sun or partial shade
SOIL Moist
GOOD ASSOCIATES *Mahonia aquifolium*, spring bulbs, *Helleborus foetidus*, *H. orientalis*, red plants generally

USE *Coloured stems in winter*

A single bush of *Cornus alba* 'Sibirica' (above), placed for impact as you turn into the garden, or as a focal point in the view from your window, can make a lasting impression – I know one did on me, just as my interest in gardening was awakening. The coloured winter stems of this cornus also have a dramatic effect in a winter arrangement.

Display your cornus against a solid background – a wall or an evergreen hedge. Surround it with other reds, to reflect and enhance the colour of its stems. Add a *Mahonia aquifolium* (keeping it low-clipped), some blue scillas, anemones and crocus, and you will have a lively winter-into-spring pageant.

This shrub needs a rich moisture-retentive soil. Once it is established, you should cut the old growth back to the main stem each spring just before the leaf buds swell. The new growth of stems will be a deep, lustrous, shining red, and on many plants the mid-green leaves also turn to red in autumn.

VIBURNUM TINUS

Laurustinus

Evergreen shrubs
White flowers, pink in bud

Moderately to very hardy
SIZE Soon reaches 3ft (90cm), ultimate
height 10ft (3m)
ASPECT From full sun to medium shade
SOIL Any moist well-drained soil
GOOD ASSOCIATES A summer-flowering
climber, such as sweet pea, eccremocarpus
or maurandia, to grow through

USE *Flowers in winter, leaves throughout*
the year

Viburnum tinus was one of the first winter-flowering shrubs to impress me: many years ago I saw a pair growing either side of a pretty Georgian front door in a village street. They were sited, as this viburnum should always be, just where the winter sun would light up the flowers.

This shrub flowers well all winter, with pink buds which open white, and you may also get blue-black berries in autumn. It is usually grown as a specimen shrub, but it can also be used as a hedge, or as an ingredient in a mixed hedge when severe clipping is not necessary. I recommend particularly 'Eve Price', with attractive carmine buds and leaves rather smaller than the type (making for a more solid effect), and the small form 'Gwellian', also with good flowers.

Viburnum leaves do not shine enough to make it a shrub for all seasons, and if it is in a prominent position it needs something growing through it to lift it in summer.

ILEX

Holly

Evergreen or deciduous shrubs
Green or variegated leaves; red or
yellow berries

Very hardy
SIZE 5–7ft (1.5–2m) after 5 years
ASPECT All do best in sun; they will
grow in shade, but less densely
SOIL Any good garden soil

USE *Leaves and berries in winter. They*
last well in water.

No flower arranger's garden should be without a holly bush. The leaves make a dark and defined background for winter flowers from the garden or the florist. I particularly like *Ilex × ataclarensis* 'Golden King', which has almost spineless leaves with broad yellow margins; and despite its name it is female, so it also has the advantage of berries. It is a fast-growing shrub, putting on as much as 16in (40cm) a year, or even more in good soil.

I. aquifolium 'Silver Queen' is another holly which makes a good splash of colour in the garden. This one is a male, so has no berries, but its leaves are prettily marked, with grey marbling and whitish margins. *I. aquifolium* 'J.C. van Tol' again has almost spineless leaves, of a dark glossy green, and the females bear an abundance of red berries. The most reliable holly for yellow berries is *I. aquifolium* 'Bacciflava'. *I. aquifolium* 'Mme Briot' (below) has leaves edged with gold.

Hollies can be clipped at any time of year – but take care to cut immediately above, not through, each leaf.

COTONEASTER

Deciduous or evergreen shrubs
Red, orange or yellow berries

Moderately to very hardy
SIZE From low-spreading forms
to 10ft (3m)
ASPECT Sun or partial shade
SOIL Any soil will do
GOOD ASSOCIATES Spring bulbs beneath
deciduous varieties

USE *Berries in autumn*

There is a cotoneaster for every position in the garden: some can be grown as ground cover, others on a wall, others as free-standing shrubs. The following are particularly useful, both in the garden and for the flower arranger. *Cotoneaster dammeri* is a spreading evergreen shrub which is good as ground cover for difficult areas of the garden, on banks, under trees, and on stony ground, and produces a reliable show of bright red berries. *C.* 'Skogholm', with orange berries, is also good evergreen ground cover, as is *C. × hybridus pendulus* (above). The deciduous *C. horizontalis* is another accommodating shrub – it will cover an ugly manhole or find its way up a wall – and is so vigorous that a few branches cut to take indoors will not be noticed.

The evergreen *C. salicifolius* 'Autumn Fire' has orange-red fruits, and a few of the leaves turn a lovely red in autumn. For yellow berries, choose the tall evergreen *C.* 'Rothschildianus' and use it either as a plant for the back of the border or as a focal point of a mixed hedge.

KOLKWITZIA AMABILIS
Beauty bush

Deciduous shrub
Pale pink flowers

Moderately to very hardy
SIZE 5ft (1.5m) after 5 years, ultimate
height up to 12ft (3.5m)
ASPECT Prefers full sun, but will flower in
partial shade
SOIL Good, well drained
GOOD ASSOCIATES Annual sweet peas or
autumn-flowering clematis, to
grow through

USE *Flowers in late spring and early*
summer, seed heads in autumn
and winter

The beauty bush makes a lovely arching
spray of soft pink flowers with a vanishing
touch of yellow in their throats. They come
into flower in late spring or early summer,
just when we are all waiting for the annual
outburst of roses and other herbaceous
excitements. Later, when the flowers turn to
seed heads, they are almost as attractive.

However, I do sometimes hear kolkwitzias
criticized for failing to flower, so when you
buy yours choose a specimen which is already showing buds or flowers. It can be
grown as a free-standing shrub or against a
wall. Prune it well after flowering, cutting
some of the old wood to ground level, and
you will have a splendid bush with enough
flowers to provide an abundant garden display and lots of cutting material.

PRUNUS
Flowering cherry

Ornamental trees and shrubs
Pink to white flowers

Very hardy
SIZE 3–26ft (1–8m)
ASPECT Sun or light shade
SOIL Any soil will do
GOOD ASSOCIATES White narcissus,
pink tulips

USE *Blossom in winter and spring*

Most flowering cherries are too large for a
small garden, or else have too short a
flowering period to be worthy of their space.
There are, however, a few exceptions.

Prunus mume, the Japanese apricot, has
pink, almond-scented double flowers in late
winter and early spring. The variant *P. mume*
'Beni-shi-don' is particularly fragrant. Keep
the small tree in shape and restrict its size by
picking liberally for your arrangements.

Another of my favourites is the winter-
flowering *P. subhirtella* 'Autumnalis', whose
white flowers appear over a period from late
autumn to early spring. *P. subhirtella*
'Pendula' (below) has pale pink flowers
covering weeping branches in spring.

I also like the purple-leaved *P. × cistena*,
which is especially effective clipped into a
low hedge. A few sprigs of this add weight to
a summer vase.

And many years ago I bought a tiny dwarf
almond called *P. tenella*, which has single
pink flowers. Cutting its 2½ft (75cm)
flowering shoots for indoor use encourages
further growth.

SYRINGA
Lilac

Deciduous shrubs
Flowers in white, cream, primrose, blue,
lilac, pink, carmine, purple

Very hardy
SIZE 3–20ft (1–6m)
ASPECT Full sun or light shade
SOIL All prefer chalk, but will tolerate
most soils; some dislike alkaline soil
GOOD ASSOCIATES *Rosa* 'Canary Bird',
Jacob's Ladder, *Thalitrum speciosum*

USE *Flowers in summer*

There must be a lilac to suit every garden. A
good nursery will be able to help you with
advice on which will be best for yours. The
following are some of my personal
favourites. For the front of the border I like
Syringa velutina (palibiniana), the Korean
lilac. It has a low, dense, compact habit with
satisfying dark green leaves, and carries
many small panicles of scented lilac-pink
flowers. Varieties for the middle of the
border include *S. × josiflexa* 'Bellicent', with
its huge panicles of rose pink. *S. vulgaris*
(above), the common lilac, which can reach
17ft (5m), is best at the back of the border, or
used as a single specimen shrub.

You should carefully prune and dead-
head your lilacs in late spring or early
summer, and remove all suckers.

ASTRANTIA
Masterwort

Herbaceous perennials
White, pink or green flowers

Very hardy
SIZE 2–3ft (60–90cm)
ASPECT Sun or partial shade
SOIL Well drained
GOOD ASSOCIATES *Malva alcea* 'Fastigiata';
pink, blue or mauve flowers

USE *Flowers all through the summer,*
dried flowers in winter

Astrantias are plants for the middle of the border. Their attractive, mound-forming basal leaves appear early in spring. The flowers are beautiful in a quiet way – 1–2in (2.5–5cm) across and perfectly symmetrical. There are several flower heads on each stem, and each flower has a tight bunch of florets surrounded by a collar of bracts. The bracts later become papery and are easily dried. I recommend *Astrantia major*, which has white florets with greenish bracts, and *A. maxima* (above), where the whole effect, in rosette and collar, is of pink.

Astrantias increase by underground runners; if you wish to confine your clumps you should dig and divide them every second year. They never require staking.

ROSA
Rose

Shrubs and climbers
Flowers of every colour except true blue

Moderately hardy
SIZE From miniature to 30ft (9m)
ASPECT Most do best in full sun
SOIL Rich, well drained
GOOD ASSOCIATES Clematis with climbers, ground cover such as violas under shrub and bush roses

USE *Flowers in summer and autumn,*
with some varieties also into winter

My preference for the garden is to plant the old-fashioned roses – Gallicas, Damasks, Bourbons and Hybrid Perpetuals. Though these old roses may not last very long in water, when massed in a vase they make for one passing hour a wonderful billowing display of soft shades and textures. However, I know that there are many flower arrangers who prefer the stiffer, more formal, and longer-lasting charms of the modern hybrids. With roses perhaps more than any other flower, any selection will always be very personal. I have selected a few of *my* favourites in various colours.

Of the old roses I am particularly fond of the climbers 'Aimée Vibert', with clusters of white flowers, and 'Zéphirine Drouhin', which is almost thornless with cerise-pink blooms; the white Bourbon 'Boule de Neige', the Gallica 'Camaieux' which has crimson-purple petals splashed with white, and the Damask 'Ispahan' (top right) with heavily scented pink flowers.

There are not many white Hybrid Teas, but I recommend 'Pascali' and the Floribunda 'Iceberg' (centre right) for cutting. Among the yellows, the Hybrid Teas 'King's Ransom' and 'Grandpa Dickson' and the cluster-flowered Floribunda 'Mountbatten' are good strong colours, and we must not forget the modern shrub roses, 'Buff Beauty', 'Penelope' and 'Golden Wings'. For pinks, the pale Floribunda 'Lady Sylvia' is wonderful for picking, and so is the bright pink, many-petalled 'Heidi'. The perfect tiny blooms of 'Cécile Brunner' are ideal for buttonholes and small bedside posies. Among the reds, the Hybrid Teas 'Alec's Red' and 'Velvet Hour' are attractive colours and last well in water.

Many roses, particularly the Rugosas (bottom right), produce beautiful hips which can be included in autumnal arrangements.

113

NERINE BOWDENII

Bulbs
Pink flowers

Moderately hardy
SIZE 2¼ft (70cm)
ASPECT Sunny and sheltered
SOIL Any good garden soil
GOOD ASSOCIATES Spring bulbs, climbing
roses, clematis

USE *Flowers in late summer and*
early autumn

The flower spikes of nerines come through
in late summer, before the leaves appear:
each stem bears a loose raceme of pale pink
flowers. Providing a burst of colour when
most other plants have finished flowering,
or are nearing the end of their season, they
are quite invaluable.

Nerines love the sun, and they need a warm
spot – a position under an exposed sunny
wall is ideal. They flower best when left
undisturbed. Dig the soil deeply and incorporate well-rotted manure before you plant
the bulbs, 6in (15cm) deep (measure from the
top of the bulb itself, and ignore the long thin
neck). A liquid feed or a dose of bonemeal
given each year before the leaves fade will
boost the bulbs. When eventually they become overcrowded, they will push their way
to the surface. This is the signal to dig them
up and replant them, a job to be done after
the leaves have died down in late spring.

HELLEBORUS

Hellebore, Christmas rose, stinking
hellebore, Lenten rose

Evergreen perennials
Flowers in white or pale green through
pink to dark burgundy

Moderately to very hardy
SIZE 1–2½ft (30–75cm)
ASPECT Sun in winter, shade in summer
SOIL Woodland or fertile garden soil
GOOD ASSOCIATES Early spring bulbs

USE *Flowers from midwinter to spring*

For me, hellebores are in a class of their own.
They make a beautiful contribution from
midwinter until the flush of spring flowers.
But remember that the 'petals' are really
sepals. You can pick the heads quite young if
you intend to float them in water, but if you
want them to last as cut flowers on longer
stems, you must wait for the sepals to age and
become papery.

It is a joy to watch the large white flowers
of *Helleborus niger*, the Christmas rose, push
through its wonderful dark leaves in midwinter. The flowers flush with pink as they
age. *H. foetidus*, the stinking hellebore, is
handsome all through the year, but makes a
striking impact in winter. Its flowers, carried
in small clusters on stems grown the previous year, are green with a red edge. *H.
corsicus*, the tallest hellebore, is a beautiful
shrubby plant that will do well in sun or
shade. The flowers of *H. orientalis* (below),
the Lenten rose, which appear in very early
spring, range in colour from white through
pink to rich plum.

DAHLIA

Herbaceous perennials with
tuberous roots
Flowers of every colour except blue

Tender; neither the tops nor the tubers
are frost-hardy, and tubers must be over-
wintered in a frost-free place
SIZE 1½–5ft (50–150cm)
ASPECT Full sun
SOIL Rich, deeply dug and well manured
GOOD ASSOCIATES *Artemisia lactiflora*

USE *Flowers from summer until frost*

With wide variations in height, colour and
size of bloom, dahlias can be suited to many
positions in the border, and used in many
different flower arrangements. The variety
'Nijinski' is illustrated above.

For best results and plenty of blooms,
prepare the site in autumn, adding manure
generously. In the spring, start your tubers
into growth in boxes, kept in a greenhouse or
other frost-proof place. When the shoots
start to grow, allow only four or five to
develop. Remove the rest and use them for
propagation, treating them as cuttings.
Transplant the tubers carefully into their
flowering positions in early summer, staking
the tall varieties when you plant them.

Alternatively, plant the tubers in
flowering position in early spring, burying
them 5in (13cm) deep, but beware of late
frost, which would damage young growth.

LONICERA
Honeysuckle (summer-flowering)

Deciduous or semi-evergreen climbing shrubs
White, yellow, red or purple flowers

Moderately to very hardy
SIZE Variable, but under good conditions some can grow to 30ft (9m)
ASPECT Light shade
SOIL Any good garden soil
GOOD ASSOCIATES Rosemary and other scented plants

USE *Flowers from late spring to autumn*

Summer-flowering honeysuckles are usually the first climber to find a place in the garden. If you have the space you can grow several, to flower from spring into autumn. The deciduous *Lonicera periclymenum* 'Belgica' produces its flowers (reddish-purple fading to yellow) in the late spring. The flowers of *L. japonica* 'Halliana', which are white changing to yellow, and the flushed purple flowers of *L. japonica repens* (both semi-evergreen) appear at midsummer, as do the flowers of the deciduous *L × americana*, which are white changing to deep yellow. *L. periclymenum* 'Serotina' (above), the late Dutch honeysuckle, also deciduous, produces rich reddish-purple flowers in the autumn.

All these are very fragrant. I would also recommend two unscented summer-flowering honeysuckles: *L.* 'Dropmore Scarlet', which has bright scarlet flowers; and *L. tragophylla*, with bright golden whorls.

Honeysuckles are best allowed to ramble at will rather than being strictly tutored.

DIANTHUS
Garden pink, border carnation

Evergreen perennials
White, pink or red flowers

Moderately to very hardy
SIZE 6–24in (15–60cm)
ASPECT Prefers sun, tolerates partial shade
SOIL Well drained
GOOD ASSOCIATES Tulips, early spring bulbs such as *Iris reticulata*

USE *Flowers in summer*

Pinks and carnations look attractive in the border, where their narrow evergreen leaves make blue-grey hummocks, and they are excellent for cutting.

The pinks are derived from *Dianthus plumarius*, and most of them are very sweet-scented. I would recommend the named varieties 'Mrs Sinkins', 'Thomas', 'Dad's Favourite', all double-flowered, and a single red, 'Brympton Red'. They flower in the earlier part of the summer. The clove carnations, which are mostly derived from *D. caryophyllus*, flower a little later. Grow them as edging, spilling over a pathway or between the cracks in a stone patio. One of my favourites is 'Nancy Lindsay' (below), and I also like the 'Highland Hybrids'.

Sow seeds of pinks or border carnations in boxes in spring, and plant them out in early summer. Increase your stock by taking heel cuttings towards the end of summer.

D. barbatus, sweet williams, are less hardy, and are best treated as biennials. Sow the seed in summer and plant out in autumn or spring. They are long-lasting in water.

SEDUM 'AUTUMN JOY'
Stonecrop

Hardy perennials
Pink flowers that turn rust-coloured as they fade

Extremely hardy
SIZE 2–3ft (60–90cm)
ASPECT Sun or partial shade
SOIL Moist but well drained
GOOD ASSOCIATES Plants with blue flowers and grey leaves, such as caryopteris

USE *Flowers in autumn, dried flowers in winter*

Stonecrops are among the most useful of perennial plants, and *Sedum* 'Autumn Joy', with small starry flowers massed into glorious heads, is perhaps the best of all the taller stonecrops. The grey-green leaf buds come through the soil in spring, and the strong stems are soon covered with fleshy leaves, to be topped in late summer by large flat pink flower heads that are very attractive to butterflies. The flowers are equally lovely in autumn, as they fade from pink to bronze to copper. And thus they remain unless they are beaten down by the snow.

They make good plants for the front of the border, especially in association with blue flowers which complement their colour range. They require no staking if you do not let the clumps grow too big – remember to divide them every other year. They are easily increased from leaf cuttings, and the stems you cut for your vases will often make roots in water and can subsequently be planted outside in spring and early summer.

PRIMULA
Primrose, polyanthus

Herbaceous perennials with evergreen leaves
Flowers of almost every colour

Moderately to very hardy
SIZE 4in–2¼ft (10–70cm)
ASPECT Sun or partial shade
SOIL Neutral to alkaline, rich, moisture-retentive
GOOD ASSOCIATES Azaleas and rhododendrons, early dwarf narcissus and species tulips

USE *Flowers from early spring into summer*

Primroses and polyanthus are the real heralds of spring. They are lovely in small arrangements, and you can pick freely from them. My choices for spring picking would be Barnhaven primulas in a wide colour range, but particularly dark maroon, the 'Gold Lace' polyanthus, patterned with gold, and *Primula* 'Garryarde Guinevere' with bronzy-purple foliage. *P. polyneura* (above), flowers at the beginning of summer. Later in summer come *P. florindae* and the candelabra primroses, which need a boggy soil to do well. Their 2¼ft (70cm) stems are dramatic in winter, with straw-coloured seed heads standing above browning leaves.

You can easily increase your stock by division or from seed. Divide established clumps after the flowers fade. Sow seed as soon as it is ripe, in a prepared seed bed in light shade. The plants can go into their permanent positions in the autumn.

ACANTHUS SPINOSUS
Bear's breeches

Herbaceous perennials
Pale mauve to purple flowers

Moderately to very hardy
SIZE 4–5ft (120–150cm)
ASPECT Sunny
SOIL Fertile, well drained
GOOD ASSOCIATES Daffodils, tulips, *Monarda* 'Prairie Night', *Hydrangea villosa*, gypsophila

USE *Leaves in spring; flower spikes fresh in summer, dried in winter. Exceptionally prickly to handle.*

The architectural quality and strength of acanthus makes it invaluable in the border and for bold flower arrangements. Its finely cut glossy green leaves are among the first to come through in spring, when they are good as a foil to late daffodils and pale tulips. By midsummer the flower spikes have developed into 3ft (90cm) spires, each with a dark purple head and a pale mauve tube. Three or five in a vase will be enough. Later in the summer the flowers mature and the seeds form, ripen until they have a dried texture, and retain their prickly elegance throughout the winter.

Plant in spring – planted in winter, the thick, fleshy roots are apt to rot off. It is wise to stake each individual spike, or the wind will soon spoil their symmetry. Plant them where they will have space to grow, and avoid disturbing your main clump if you possibly can. Once your acanthus are established, they will spread by suckers.

ASTER
Michaelmas daisy

Herbaceous perennials
Lavender-blue, violet, pink or bright rose flowers

Very hardy
SIZE 1⅓–4½ft (40–140cm)
ASPECT Sunny (they grow leggy in shade)
SOIL Any good garden soil
GOOD ASSOCIATES Sedum, gypsophila, *Artemisia* 'Powis Castle'

USE *Flowers in late summer. They last well in water.*

Asters, in their many shades, are very useful to both gardeners and flower arrangers. Decide what colour you want to blend into your borders, and also to suit your colour schemes indoors.

Be sure to buy the best varieties. A good selection is *Aster × frikartii* (3ft, 90cm), with light lavender-blue flowers; the violet *A. amellus* 'King George' (above, only 2ft, 60cm); *A. novae-angliae* 'Harrington's Pink' (4ft, 120cm) and *A. novae-angliae*. 'Alma Potschke' (3¼ft, 100cm), whose startling bright rose-pink flowers need a grey neighbour to soothe and bring out their wonderful colour. The hybrids do vary in hardiness, so it is worth checking when you buy plants that they are suitable for your area.

Most asters become untidy at their base as summer advances – hide their lower stems with front-row plants such as gypsophila, sedum or artemisia. Increase your stock by division or by taking young shoots from the edges of your clumps, in spring.

PULMONARIA
Lungwort, soldiers and sailors

Perennial ground cover
Pink and blue flowers; green leaves,
spotted with grey

Extremely hardy
SIZE 12in (30cm)
ASPECT Full or partial shade
SOIL Any good garden soil
GOOD ASSOCIATES Chionodoxas, scillas,
snowdrops, Solomon's seal

USE *Leaves during most of the year,*
flowers in winter and spring

I consider pulmonarias essential winter-flowering plants. Their grey-spotted leaves also make ideal ground cover for most of the year. The stems, leaves and flower cups are covered with silky hairs which shine in the sun. They deserve a shady home at the front of a border or beside a path, where they can be enjoyed at close quarters.

The common name 'soldiers and sailors' derives from the mixture of pink and blue flowers, while 'lungwort' stems from a supposed similarity between the spots on the leaves and lung disease. To me they are a truly cottage garden plant. *Pulmonaria officinalis* (below) has narrow, white-spotted leaves. *P. saccharata* has silver-white blotches. *P. saccharata* 'Mrs Moon' and *P. saccharata* 'Margery Fish' are good cultivars; there are blue and white forms too.

Cut off all the flowering stems after the plants have flowered, to give the new leaves space to develop freely. Increase your stock by division, after flowering.

SCABIOSA CAUCASICA
Scabious, pincushion flower

Herbaceous perennials
Blue flowers

Extremely hardy
SIZE 2–2¼ft (60–70cm)
ASPECT Full sun in temperate
climates, light shade where the summers
are very hot
SOIL Light, loamy, alkaline rather
than acid
GOOD ASSOCIATES *Physostegia virginiana*

USE *Flowers all through the summer*

This plant has pretty-petalled frilly flowers 4in (10cm) across, usually powdery blue or lavender. The flower stems are almost leafless. William Robinson considered it the finest perennial in his garden. Plant them in largish clumps for a grand effect, and to have plenty of flowers to pick from early summer to the first days of autumn. *Scabiosa caucasica* 'Clive Greaves' is the best, with pale lavender-blue flowers; 'Miss Willmott' is a beautiful creamy white.

Scabious flower over a long period and repay constant dead-heading; no staking is needed. You can grow them from seed, but the named cultivars must be bought as plants and then increased by division. You should divide and replant every other spring, as the old plants will deteriorate and die out.

CLEMATIS

Deciduous or evergreen climbing shrubs
Flowers of every colour

Moderately to very hardy
SIZE Up to 20ft (6m)
ASPECT Most like sun, with shaded roots,
but some will tolerate shade
SOIL Alkaline, rich, and moist but
well drained
GOOD ASSOCIATES Roses, other deciduous
and evergreen shrubs

USE *Flowers during most of the year*

The small blooms of the clematis that flower during spring and autumn are useful for posies; while the huge flowers produced by summer-flowering hybrids such as 'Nelly Moser' and 'Lasurstern' look lovely floating in shallow bowls of water.

In the garden, clematis will climb on walls and fences or scramble through other shrubs. They like a deep root-run, and hate getting too dry. If you intend to grow a clematis up a wall, plant it 12in (30cm) away and train the stems back. Always plant deeper than the pot level – this helps to prevent wilt – and avoid disturbing the roots. Protect the fragile young stems during the first season.

Clematis of the Jackmanii (below), Texensis and Viticella groups, which flower in late summer and autumn on new wood, need to be pruned hard in early spring. The spring-flowering Alpinas, Macropetalas and Montanas need minimal pruning, just enough to keep them neat, and I also find it best to leave the large-flowered hybrids alone, except for a gentle spring tidy.

VIOLA
Pansy, violet, viola

Herbaceous perennials, hardy annuals or biennials
Flowers of almost every colour except strong red and green

Moderately to very hardy
SIZE 4–20in (10–50cm)
ASPECT Sun or partial shade
SOIL Any fertile soil
GOOD ASSOCIATES Roses

USE *Flowers in spring and summer*

Pansies, violets and violas are small plants of great charm, their 'faces' among the most varied and amusing in the garden, their scents among the most delicious. Grow them as edging, under shrubs, especially roses, and running through other plants. They are delightful in small arrangements. *Viola cornuta* is illustrated above.

Pansies come in almost any colour, or with distinct markings. They are best grown from seed – treated as annuals or biennials – or bought as trays of seedlings. Sown in trays or outside in a seed bed at midsummer, spring pansies will be ready to be put out in their flowering positions by late autumn. The summer-flowering pansies can be sown in early spring. When you have established a favourite you can increase it by cuttings.

Many of the violets and violas come true from seed, but for some of the older and more cherished varieties you should propagate by taking cuttings.

NIGELLA DAMASCENA
Love-in-a-mist

Hardy annuals
Pale blue flowers

Moderately to very hardy
SIZE 1¾–2¼ft (50–70cm)
ASPECT Prefers sun, but will tolerate light shade
SOIL Any well-cultivated garden soil
GOOD ASSOCIATES Heucheras, ferns, *Alchemilla mollis*, grey foliage plants, plants with white, pink or pale yellow flowers

USE *Flowers throughout the summer, seed heads later*

Nigella is among the easiest of annuals to grow, and is attractive in all its stages. The blue flowers, each with its collarette of narrow, fennel-like leaves, are very pretty, and the round seed heads, green at first then drying to straw colour, are good for winter vases. Annuals like nigella are particularly useful to clothe new borders while shrubs or perennials are maturing.

Sow the seeds where they are to flower, in early spring or in autumn, and thin the seedlings to 6–8in (15–20cm) apart. Sown in spring, they will flower in late summer; sown in autumn, they will generally survive the winter and be ready to flower in early summer. Alternatively, you can sow two or three seeds into small pots in autumn and over-winter them in a frame to plant outside in spring (being careful not to disturb the roots). The flowers will supply you with self-sown seedlings, so weed cautiously.

AGAPANTHUS
Blue African lily

Herbaceous perennials
Dark blue to pale blue or white flowers

Moderately hardy
SIZE 2–4ft (60–120cm)
ASPECT Full sun
SOIL Fertile, moist
GOOD ASSOCIATES *Nerine bowdenii*, spring bulbs; grey foliage plants such as santolina, *Artemisia* 'Powis Castle', *Artemisia ludoviciana*

USE *Flowers in late summer, seed heads in winter*

I think of agapanthus as front-row plants, grown in drifts. The flower spikes tend to lean towards the sun, so plant them in an exposed, light border.

Several strains that are reliably hardy are now available. Those with narrow leaves are generally hardier than the broad-leaved varieties, but these, which are often ever-green, will over-winter happily in a tub in a frost-free place. The Headbourne hybrids (above) are the hardiest agapanthus, and they are less expensive than the named forms, but colours and heights will be unspecified.

Left undisturbed, clumps develop slowly in a temperate climate, rather more quickly where the summers are hot. Increase by division in spring. If you allow some seed heads to remain as winter silhouettes, you can expect seedlings.

CAMPANULA
Bellflower

Herbaceous perennials
Blue or white flowers

Moderately to very hardy
SIZE 8in–5ft (20–150cm)
ASPECT Sun or shade
SOIL Fertile, well drained
GOOD ASSOCIATES *Coreopsis verticillata* for
low varieties, pink roses for taller ones,
Sedum 'Ruby Glow'

USE *Flowers through summer and autumn*

A garden, however small, without some
campanulas is unthinkable. The following
varieties would be my choice for flower
arranging. *Campanula carpatica* and *C.
muralis*, both with neat tufts of leaves and a
profusion of flowers, are excellent for edging
and the corner of the border. C. 'Burghaltii',
with large grey-lilac flowers, can be hard to
find, but is worth seeking out. *C. glomerata*
'Superba', 20in (50cm) tall, with violet-
purple flowers in rounded heads, is particularly good for cutting. It can be invasive, so
put it with another invader, such as
Artemisia ludoviciana. *C. persicifolia*, blue or
white, a favourite since the sixteenth cen-
tury, will flower all summer on 3ft (90cm)
stems, but you must have the patience to
dead-head often. *C. lactiflora* (below) bears
bell-shaped flowers on 3–5ft (90–150cm)
branching stems. The tall chimney
bellflower, *C. pyramidalis*, is wonderful
grown in pots and brought into the house,
where the white or blue flowers and heart-
shaped leaves will last for weeks.

ROSMARINUS
Rosemary

Evergreen shrubs
Pale to deep blue flowers; grey-green
leaves

Very hardy
SIZE 2½–4ft (75–120cm)
ASPECT Full sun
SOIL Light, well drained
GOOD ASSOCIATES White clematis,
spring bulbs

USE *Leaves throughout the year, flowers*
in spring

No garden should be without a rosemary.
You can have it as a specimen shrub in the
front or back of the border, use it on a sunny
wall, or make a low hedge with it. Pictures of
medieval gardens sometimes show rosemary
used for topiary. The aromatic sprays of
narrow evergreen leaves make a lovely addition to vases at any time of the year, and in
spring you also have the pleasure of the
pretty blue flowers. It is also, of course, a
pungent flavouring herb.

I particularly like the common rosemary,
Rosmarinus officinalis (above), one of the best
for flavouring, and among the hardiest; the
dwarf shrub *R. officinalis* 'Severn Sea', with
deep blue flowers; and the gilded rosemary,
R. officinalis 'Follis Aureus'. *R.* 'Miss
Jessup's Upright' is difficult to find, but
makes an attractive narrow pyramid.

Provided you plant rosemary in full sun,
in a well-drained soil which never gets waterlogged, it is surprisingly adaptable. Most
varieties take easily from cuttings.

DELPHINIUM
Delphinium, larkspur

Herbaceous perennials or hardy annuals
Flowers of every colour

Extremely hardy
SIZE 2–7ft (60cm–2m)
ASPECT Sunny
SOIL Rich, well cultivated and
well drained, alkaline rather than acid
GOOD ASSOCIATES Grey-leaved
plants, nepeta

USE *Flowers from the middle to the end*
of summer

The tall blue *Delphinium elatum* is the main
parent of the familiar garden hybrids.
Named varieties range in colour from white,
cream and pale yellow to strong blues,
mauves and purples – in fact, a colour for
every arrangement. There is also a height for
every border.

Provided named plants are protected from
their chief enemies, slugs and snails, they
will give you good spikes from their first
year. Grown from seed, delphiniums take
two seasons fully to develop, but once
established they will last for many seasons.
Give a boost of bonemeal in early spring, and
be sure to stake your spikes carefully, or a
sudden gust of strong wind may lay them all
flat. Cuttings may be sliced from the parent
plant in spring.

D. ajacis (below), larkspur, is among the
most rewarding of annuals, especially if you
can spare the space for a bold group. Removing the flowering spikes before they set seed
will encourage a second crop of flowers.

MUSCARI
Grape hyacinth

Bulbs
White to blue flowers

Moderately to very hardy
SIZE 5–8in (13–20cm)
ASPECT Sunny
SOIL Well drained
GOOD ASSOCIATES Violets, dwarf narcissus,
aubrieta, species tulips, taller red tulips,
later herbaceous plants or hardy annuals

USE *Flowers in spring*

Grape hyacinths are among the most reliable
of the spring bulbs, and their strong, stiff
stems make them excellent for cutting.
Muscari armeniacum (above) has fragrant,
bright blue flowers, M. *azureum* paler blue,
early-flowering blooms; and there is a white
form, M. *botryoides* 'Album'. They are lovely
edging a pathway, on the perimeter of woodland, or under deciduous trees, especially
flowering cherries. We have them unfurling
like blue ribbons in narrow beds, with *Viola*
'Mauve Haze' spread generously between
them to cover their leaves as they die. In a
small garden you can tuck them away between herbaceous plants which will eventually spread around them, or sow hardy
annuals among them.

Grape hyacinths require very little attention. Just plant the bulbs 4in (10cm) deep –
and take care not to damage the young leaves
when they come through in late autumn. Left
to themselves, they will increase rapidly.

IRIS

Bulbs and rhizomes
Flowers of every colour except bright red

Moderately to very hardy
SIZE 4–14in (10–35cm)
ASPECT Most need sun
SOIL There are irises for most soils: check
particular requirements before planting
GOOD ASSOCIATES Snowdrops and low
ground cover plants for *Iris reticulata*;
peonies, lilies and annual poppies for flag
irises; santolina for Dutch irises

USE *Flowers in winter, spring and*
summer

There is an iris for almost every season of the
year. At the start of winter *Iris unguicularis* (I.
stylosa) opens its exquisite rich lavender
flowers. Pick them in bud and bring them
indoors to unfold and release their scent. In
late winter and early spring comes *I.*
reticulata (below), in various shades of purple. A few nestled with snowdrops in a
shallow bowl filled with moss are a joy.

In early summer come the Dutch irises,
with strong stems and sturdy flowers, ranging from white to yellow, blue to purple.
They are best planted in a position where
there will be no big gaps when you cut them.

The summer-flowering flag irises are tall,
majestic flowers which make a splendid
effect in an arrangement. Carefully break off
each bloom as it fades and the next one will
open. They should be planted with their
rhizomes just showing, so they get a good
baking during the hot months. Divide and
move them in late summer.

NEPETA
Catmint, catnip

Herbaceous perennials
Lavender flowers; grey leaves

Extremely hardy
SIZE 1ft or 3ft (30cm or 90cm)
ASPECT Sun
SOIL Well drained
GOOD ASSOCIATES Peonies, white and
pink roses

USE *Flowering sprays in summer*

In flower arrangements nepeta is the back-up
– the chorus, not the prima donna. The
attractive lavender blooms and grey leaves
blend well with most colours and if you cut
the stems, others will grow. In the garden it is
excellent as an edging, especially where it can
spill unchecked over a path; and its small,
soft, grey leaves make a good summer
ground cover in beds.

The two best catmints are *Nepeta faassenii*
(N. × *mussinii*), growing only to 12in (30cm),
which is wonderful for edging and for
ground cover in rose beds, and N. 'Six Hills
Giant', which grows to 36in (90cm) and
associates very well with herbaceous plants,
especially peonies.

Cut back the stems of nepeta after the first
flowering, and you will get a second
flowering in late summer. After that, allow
the dead stems to stay on for the winter, to
give the plant some protection from frost.
Increase in spring, by division or by cuttings.

HOSTA
Plantain lily

Herbaceous perennials
White or pale mauve flowers; leaves in
many shades, and often variegated

Very hardy
SIZE 6in–5ft (15–150cm)
ASPECT Light shade
SOIL Rich, moist
GOOD ASSOCIATES Daffodils, tulips, ferns,
epimediums, plants with
narrow, sword-like leaves, for example,
hemerocallis, crocosmia

USE *Leaves in spring and summer,*
flowers in summer, dried leaves in winter

There are many beautiful varieties of hostas
to choose from. Hosta leaves come in green,
grey, blue, centred or edged with white,
yellow or lime green. They vary in size from
2in (5cm) to 12in (30cm) across, in shape
from lance-like to rounded, and in texture
from smooth to puckered, ribbed to wavy.
In addition, many hostas have flowers that
are very attractive in appearance, or fragrant, or both.

Hostas do well in shade, but they deserve a
position where their lovely foliage can be
fully appreciated. Remember when you
place them that they will increase in size and
beauty as they mature, and they will do best
if they are left undisturbed to develop into
substantial clumps. They may need some
protection from slugs and snails, which can
ruin the leaves. Increase by seed – they can be
divided but it is best to avoid disturbing the
clumps if you can.

ALCHEMILLA MOLLIS
Lady's mantle

Herbaceous perennials
Lime-green flowers; green leaves

Moderately to very hardy
SIZE 20in (50cm)
ASPECT Sun or shade in temperate
climates; shade in hot countries
SOIL Fertile, moist
GOOD ASSOCIATES White, yellow, blue and
purple flowers; keep away from orange-
red and pink

USE *Leaves from spring to autumn,*
flowers throughout the summer, dried
flowers in winter

Graceful in flower and leaf, alchemilla combines well with almost all other flowers. The
rounded and slightly serrated grey-green
leaves appear in spring. The sprays of starry
lime-green flowers begin to push up in early
summer, and the plant will go on flowering
for at least two months.

I use alchemilla as an edging, so the leaves
soften the hard lines of paving stones. Right
up to it I plant spring bulbs, or polyanthus,
which will have finished flowering and can
be moved before the alchemilla leaves become too large.

Alchemilla seeds itself almost too profusely, and once it has filled its allotted space
it is wise to remove every flower spike before
the seeds ripen. If you shear over the whole
plant after the first flowering, then give it a
generous top-dressing of peat with
bonemeal, and a good watering, it will
produce a fresh carpet of leaves.

FERNS

Hardy ferns, mostly evergreen
Green fronds

Moderately to very hardy
SIZE 4in–2ft (10–60cm)
ASPECT Shade
SOIL Moist, not too rich
GOOD ASSOCIATES Solomon's seal,
mandrakes, pulmonarias, hostas, lilies,
spring bulbs

USE *Foliage, throughout the year*

The green elegance of fern fronds makes a
calm, pleasing background for flowers, both
in the garden and in arrangements. Gertrude
Jekyll, doyenne of gardeners, recommended
that ferns should be planted in drifts in the
woodland garden in association with lilies,
and in shady borders with groups of hostas
and spring bulbs.

For the flower arranger, I would suggest:
Adiantum pedatum, the deciduous maiden-
hair fern, with black wiry stems 20in (50cm)
long; *Asplenium scolopendrium*, the evergreen
hart's tongue fern; *Athyrium filix-femina*, the
lady fern, which likes moisture; *Dryopteris
filix-mas*, the male fern, for its ability to
thrive in dry soil; *Osmunda regalis*, the royal
fern; *Polypodium vulgare*, a great colonizer,
good for ground cover; and my favourite,
Polystichum setiferum, the soft shield fern.

Ferns are among the most trouble-free of
all plants. The majority are easily raised
from spores, and once established they will
need no attention except for an annual
removal of fading fronds.

GARRYA ELLIPTICA
Tassel bush

Evergreen shrubs
Grey-green flowers

Moderately hardy
SIZE 8ft (2.5m) after 5 years, ultimate
height 15ft (4.5m)
ASPECT Prefers full sun, but will tolerate
light shade
SOIL Fertile
GOOD ASSOCIATES Autumn-flowering
clematis or sweet peas, to grow through,
winter jasmine

USE *Catkins in winter and early spring*

This evergreen shrub can be used as a free-standing specimen or given a place on a wall. It is important to buy a male plant, as the females have less striking flowers. In summer even the male has a somewhat drab appearance, since the leaves are rather lustreless, but in winter it really comes into its own, as the exciting catkins gradually elongate to 6–8in (15–20cm).

A free-standing shrub requires no pruning, unless you want to reduce in size. If you have it on a wall, clip it back as soon as the catkins have faded – the same moment the old leaves fall and the new ones start to grow in their place.

We have this garrya on a wall facing north-west, and it does reasonably well, but it would really prefer a sunnier spot – in too much shade it becomes straggly and flowers less well. The autumn-flowering *Clematis viticella* 'Alba Luxurians' grows through it, lifting it during a drab phase.

EUONYMUS FORTUNEI
Evergreen spindle

Evergreen shrubs
Green or variegated leaves

Very hardy
SIZE 2–3ft (60–90cm), more as a climber
ASPECT Prefers sun, but will tolerate shade
SOIL Alkaline, but will tolerate any
GOOD ASSOCIATES For contrasting foliage,
rosemary, ivy or *Vitis coignetiae*

USE *Leaves throughout the year*

Years ago, long before it became widely popular, I bought the golden-leaved *Euonymus fortunei* and it has done us extremely well. Use it as an evergreen in front of the border and, with nothing to climb up, it will stay low. Give it a wall or a tree trunk and it will discover its ability to climb – in our garden, up an old pear tree.

The leaves make a wonderful addition to flower arrangements. They always have an ample supply of gold, and in very cold winters they acquire a pink tinge.

The books say 'Do not prune'. This is only half-right. You need not prune euonymus as a free-standing shrub, but if you want it to cover a wall for you, giving a solid effect, then allow it to get started and thereafter keep it pruned back to the wall; in so doing you will also have plenty of material for your arrangements.

ELEAGNUS

Deciduous or evergreen shrubs
Green leaves marked with gold, or with
silver undersides

Moderately to very hardy
SIZE About 4ft (120cm) after 5 years,
ultimate height about 10ft (3m)
ASPECT Will tolerate deep shade, keeping
coloured leaves
SOIL Any soil that is not too dry
GOOD ASSOCIATES Spring bulbs, yellow
summer flowers

USE *Coloured leaves throughout the year,*
and, with some varieties, flowers in
summer

Perhaps the most popular eleagnus, among both gardeners and flower arrangers, is *Elaeagnus pungens* 'Maculata'. Its leaves, with their bright yellow centres, positively shine out in the border, and the stiff stems form a good basis for an arrangement. *E. × ebbingei* (above) has green leaves with a silvery underside, that look very attractive in a vase. The pale yellow to silver flowers, borne on old wood in mid- to late summer, are inconspicuous in appearance, but sweetly scented. *E. × ebbingei* 'Gilt Edge' has golden margins, *E. × ebbingei* 'Limelight' a golden central blotch. *E. angustifolia* also has small but fragrant summer flowers, and so does *E. umbellata parvifolia*, which often later bears small round orange fruits.

In general eleagnus do not live much longer than ten years. They need no pruning, but with the variegated forms, remember to remove any unvariagated shoots.

HEDERA
Ivy

Evergreen climbing shrubs
Green leaves, sometimes marked with
grey or gold

Very hardy
SIZE About 5ft (150cm)
ASPECT Medium shade generally preferred,
full sun best for golden-leaved forms
SOIL Needs moisture to establish, but after
that will tolerate dry conditions
GOOD ASSOCIATES *Clematis × jackmanii*,
climbing roses

USE *Leaves throughout the year,*
fruits in autumn

The conventional use of ivy is as an evergreen climber, often hiding an unsightly shed or clothing a wall. It is self-clinging, and you can clip it and guide it in the required direction. It can also be trained as a ribbon edging a path, or used to hang down from a low retaining wall, or as a ground cover carpet. I have seen it draped over a large stone like a shawl.

There is a very wide range of size and type of variegation among ivy leaves – from the 6–8in (15–20cm) grey-green leaves of *Hedera colchica* 'Dentata Variegata', with their creamy margins, and *H. colchica* 'Sulphur Heart', splashed with yellow, to the 1in (2.5cm) leaves of *H. helix* 'Gold Heart', with a central yellow blotch, and *H. helix* 'Glacier' (below), with silver margins. These leaves are fun to use in arrangements – as sprays to drape down from a vase, or as individuals in an informal mixed posy.

EUCALYPTUS
Gum tree

Evergreen trees
Blue-grey leaves

Moderately to very hardy; frost may kill
top growth, but it will regenerate
SIZE Tall tree unless cut back to encourage
young growth
ASPECT Full sun
SOIL Well drained
GOOD ASSOCIATES *Cotinus coggygria*
'Atropurpureus'

USE *Young leaves*

I hesitate to recommend planting a eucalyptus in a small garden especially designed for the flower arranger because it is usually possible to buy eucalyptus stems from a florist. However, your own material is always better and fresher, and if you do have sufficient space it is well worth growing *Eucalyptus gunnii* (above), the cider gum, for its silver-blue young foliage (the adult leaves are quite different, sage green and a sickle shape). Or you could try *E. pauciflora* or *E. perriniana*. If you can, plant your gum tree against an evergreen hedge and the winter growth will show up particularly well.

To keep a constant supply of new growth at a height convenient for picking, you must be quite ruthless early each spring and cut all last year's growth to ground level. You will then have a good supply of young wood with attractive small, round leaves to pick for your arrangements.

VINCA MAJOR 'VARIEGATA'
Periwinkle

Evergreen perennials
Variegated green and golden leaves; blue
flowers

Very hardy
SIZE 12in (30cm)
ASPECT Sun or shade
SOIL Any good garden soil
GOOD ASSOCIATES Dark green hollies

USE *Hanging stems with variegated*
leaves. They last well in water.

This variegated vinca has very attractive leaves, on long stems. If it is to flower the stems must be cut back in winter. But if you sacrifice the flowers and allow the stems to remain on until spring, you will have good-sized sprays – each leaf prettily marked, with pale yellow edges – for your winter vases.

All the vincas make good ground cover, and this one is especially effective in shady places. We have it under deep green hollies in rather a dark corner. I have also seen it used successfully on a slightly raised bed along a driveway, growing between and through *Cotoneaster horizontalis*. It can be useful in the border too, so long as you do not give the stems an opportunity to tip root and spread all over the place.

Although tip rooting can be a nuisance, it does make increasing your stock very easy. Peg some of the ends down or just bury them under a shallow layer of soil and they will soon form roots.

Vinca minor is useful too, but the leaves are less dramatic.

GARDENING AND FLOWER ARRANGING TECHNIQUES

As you enjoy your garden in the summer, it is easy to forget about the hard work you put into it to bring it to this peak. For those who have been inspired by this book to extend their gardening endeavours, the techniques in this section – when to mulch, how to prune, where to plant and all the other essential seasonal tasks – provide some basic information you will need to create and maintain a garden of shrubs and flowers, especially those used by the flower arranger. Decorating your home with flowers and foliage from your own garden is deeply satisfying. Whether your taste is for generous bunches heaped into jugs, delicate posies, or more intricate combinations, a few guidelines about arranging techniques and equipment available will ensure that your flowers are always displayed successfully.

◆

MIDSUMMER REWARD
The richest benefits of garden toil come at the height of summer, when even an elaborate arrangement can be effortlessly furnished with antirrhinums, roses, campanula, salvia, clematis, dictamnus, philadelphus and lavatera.

PREPARING A BED OR BORDER

When planning a bed or a border there are a number of things which must be taken into account and which will inform your choices before settling on a site and choosing plants. A visit to neighbours' gardens and discussion with them will be a great help to you if you have just moved into a new house.

SOIL There are some basic facts about soil which will give a good idea of its composition. A clay soil feels sticky, becomes waterlogged easily and is slow to warm up in the spring. A sandy soil, on the other hand, dries out fast and warms up quickly in the spring. A loam soil, one which may be acid or alkaline, is a balance of humus, and of clay, sand or limestone. It possesses all the best qualities: it feels spongy underfoot, has an open texture, and is well drained.

To test the pH of the soil – its acidity or alkalinity – a simple way is to buy a kit. Your results will determine the plants that will thrive in your garden. If rhododendrons flourish this is a sure sign that the soil is acid.

ASPECT Consider how much light the proposed site will get at different times of the year, and discover how much frost the area has in order to determine which plants will be likely to survive. Degree of exposure is important too: wind is one of the elements most detrimental to plants, but often least considered as an enemy. It can rob plants of valuable moisture, rock their roots and disfigure their leaves. A dip in the ground where cold air collects will be susceptible to frost, which could damage or even destroy plants. Frost flows downhill – you can divert it in many instances by planting a hedge.

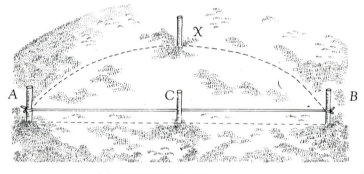

MARKING OUT AN OVAL BED

1. Mark either end of the long axis with pegs (A & B). Stretch string from A to B and knot around each peg. Mark the mid point (C), and place a peg (X) at right angles to C and at half the desired bed width.

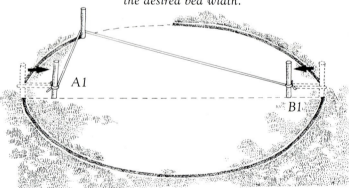

2. Move A and B equal distances in from the ends of the oval until you can loop the string around X. Hammer the pegs in here (A1 & B1). Scratch out the oval with peg X, keeping the string taut at all times.

MARKING OUT AN IRREGULAR-SHAPED BED

Take a long piece of rope approximately three times the desired length of the bed and knot the two ends together. Throw the rope down on the ground and experiment until you have the desired shape of your bed. Hammer in pegs at roughly 1m (3ft) intervals. The same method in reverse is used if you have planned the shape of your bed on graph paper. Mark out the design on the site with pegs and then link the pegs with string.

DOUBLE DIGGING

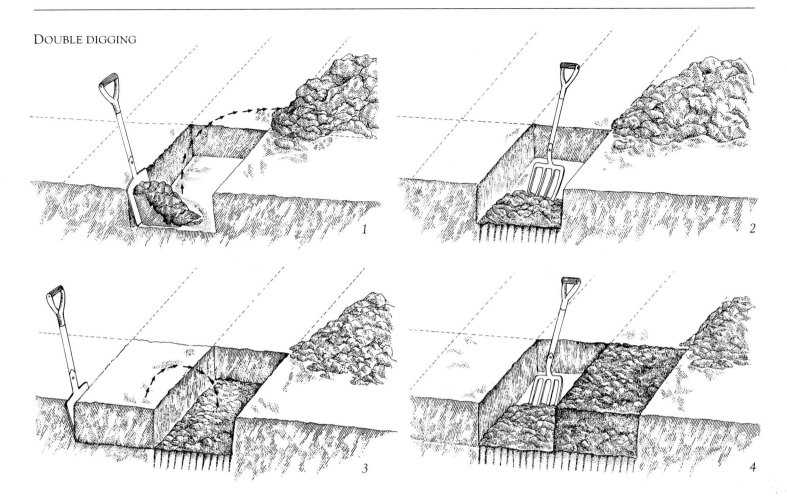

PREPARING THE SITE

Once you have chosen a site, plan the shape of the bed or border and draw it up to scale on a piece of graph paper, plotting in all the surrounding features such as borders, lawn, trees or shrubs. Transfer the finished design of your border to the proposed site using wooden pegs or bamboo canes placed at 3–4ft (1m) intervals, marking it out with string, if necessary, to define the area more accurately.

If the plot has been staked out on a piece of lawn that is well maintained and reasonably weed free, it will simply be a matter of removing the turf. Use a turfing iron to lift the turf and a half-moon tool to neaten the edges.

If you intend to use the turf elsewhere, clear it all, either stacking it neatly or laying it out on its new site. If the turf is not needed it can be put in the bottom of each trench as you dig.

Although double digging is hard work, it is absolutely essential for an area that may not be turned over again for several years. It will aerate the soil, improve soil drainage and uproot deeply embedded weed roots.

To double dig, first dig a strip at one end of the bed 2ft (60cm) wide to one spade's depth (1). Move the soil to the far end of the bed and lay it on some sacking or polythene. Break up the soil at the bottom of the trench and fork in well-rotted manure, good compost and the turf taken from the next strip (2). Dig a second strip adjacent to the first, filling the first trench with soil removed from the second (3). Fork the base of the new trench (4). Carry on to the end of the bed and fill the last trench with soil removed from the first strip.

Finally, break up any large clumps of soil and tread the surface. Sprinkle it with fertilizer – approximately two handfuls per square yard (metre) – and rake into the top few inches of soil. Leave for six weeks before planting to allow the soil to settle.

Ideally preparation should be done in autumn or winter ready for spring planting. If you are renovating a bed that has become overgrown, you must clear the area thoroughly. A combination of hoeing general surface weeds and digging deep-rooted weeds with a border fork and removing by hand should be sufficient for most areas. If the site is full of couch grass, it can be extremely difficult to remove. Try spraying with glyphosate – following the instructions carefully. Dispose of weeds by either burning them or putting them on a compost heap.

CHOOSING AND POSITIONING PLANTS

When buying a plant from a garden centre or market stall, look for tell-tale signs of an unhealthy plant: wilting or yellowing leaves, infestations of pest or disease, and any thick roots growing through the base of the container. At a good garden centre the plants should be clearly labelled, with moist soil that is weed free – but a little algae is a healthy sign. The plant that you buy should have a firm healthy top-growth and small roots peeping through the sides of the container.

If you buy plants by mail order from a nursery, you will usually have a wider choice than at a garden centre, but you will be unable to inspect the plants before buying. Order well in advance and you should have them when you want to plant.

As a general rule you get what you pay for. Bargain offers may thrive but it is more often the case that they have been poorly handled and not properly hardened off. Most plants do not recover from a bad start in life, so a little extra expenditure should guarantee a greater degree of success and pleasure.

If you are given plants, make sure before planting that they are not full of ground elder or any other nasty weeds.

PLANTING OUT

Draw up a planting plan to scale allowing for plants that might spread, their various shapes, their bulk and their height when fully grown. Consider the site from all angles. A small bed can be laid out on the site, but do not leave plants with their roots exposed for more than a few hours since wind and sun will dry out and damage roots very quickly.

If you have prepared the soil properly, it will not be necessary to add more fertilizer. The soil should feel moist when squeezed – water it if necessary. Be careful not to tread the soil too firmly while planting as this will destroy the soil structure. If possible have a wooden board to stand on: this distributes your weight and does not compact the soil as footsteps do.

The plants should also be thoroughly watered before planting. Plants that have been bought pre-packed in polythene bags may need to be soaked in a bucket of water for 2–3 hours if the roots feel dry.

Dig a hole for the plant, allowing enough space so that you can spread out the roots well. The hole should be deep enough so that the soil surface of the plant is approximately 1in (2.5cm) below ground level. Fill the base of the hole with a 2–4in (5–10cm) layer of peat and topsoil mix or a proprietary planting mixture. Tap the container against your fork handle, remove the plant and place in the hole. (If plants are bought in soft polythene containers, these should be cut off, not pulled off, to prevent root damage.) Fill the space around the soil ball with planting mixture and press down firmly.

Handle young small plants very carefully; their roots are fragile. When planting bulbs in your border use a special bulb planter or trowel.

PROPAGATION

There is nothing more satisfying in the garden than propagating your own plants. The processes involved are simple, and propagation is the cheapest and most effective means of increasing your stock and replacing old plants.

GROWING FROM SEED

To sow seeds indoors or in the greenhouse, fill a clean plastic tray or pot with a proprietary seed compost. Firm the compost down with a wooden board to create a level surface about ½in (1cm) below the rim.

Scatter the seeds evenly across the top of the container. Small seeds can be mixed with sand for a more even distribution, while larger seeds can be placed individually. Cover the seeds with a thin layer of compost. Water with a watering can fitted with a fine rose or soak the tray in a shallow bath of water. Place a sheet of glass over the container and shade with a layer of newspaper. Put the seeds in a warm place, either a heated propagator, an airing cupboard or shaded window sill, 12–18°C (54–64°F), to germinate.

Germination usually takes between one and three weeks, but some seeds can take as long as a year. Do not allow the compost to dry out.

When the seedlings begin to show, remove the covering and place the container in good light, but not direct sunlight. The seedlings, at this stage, are fragile and susceptible to disease; over-watering and overcrowding can cause damping-off. Watering with Cheshunt Compound will reduce this risk.

Prick out the seedlings once true leaves have formed. Loosen and lift them in clumps with a knife or dibber and then separate by hand, trying not to damage the root systems. Handle by the seed leaves not the stem. Fill the tray with potting compost, firm and level it and make holes, approximately 2in (5cm) apart, with a dibber. Lower the seedlings into the holes and firm into the compost. Label the tray and water in.

HARDENING OFF The young seedlings must be hardened off gradually before transferring outdoors. Move to an unheated garden frame after four to eight weeks, opening it for a few hours every day – do not place in full sun. If you do not have a frame, improvise using a window sill out of the sun. Gradually increase the seedlings' exposure to unfiltered light and air.

Once hardened off and well grown they can be planted in their final position in the garden. Delay this, if necessary, until there is no risk of frost. The ground should be prepared several days before planting out by breaking up large clods of soil to a fine tilth.

SOWING OUTDOORS Most hardy annuals can be sown outdoors in a seedbed, or directly into their position in the garden. It is most important that the soil should be well prepared: dig the site in early autumn, before the frosts, to ensure that it is level and well aerated; break down large lumps of soil with a rake. Fertilize the soil, preferably with manure, although peat, leaf mould or well decayed compost are suitable alternatives. In the spring, rake in fertilizer just before sowing, and, if the weather is dry, water the drills to speed up germination. The seeds are either sown in shallow drills formed by drawing a hoe through the soil, or simply scattered over an area and lightly raked in. A garden line stretched across the bed will ensure straight planting rows. Sow the seeds thinly, taking into account the plant's ultimate height and spread, and rake over the soil to cover them. Firm the soil lightly and label the row clearly. Water thoroughly after sowing if the weather is dry and again one week later. Thin out when the seedlings are large enough to handle easily.

CUTTINGS

This method of propagation involves taking a small piece of a mature plant to develop an independent root system. The type of cutting depends both on the kind of growth that the plant produces and on the time of year.

SOFTWOOD CUTTINGS These are taken, usually in spring or early summer, from the soft growth produced at the tip of stems during the growing season.

Cut a healthy shoot, a few inches in length, just below a leaf joint (1). Always trim the parent plant back to the next joint so that it does not die back. Carefully cut away any leaves on the lower third of the shoot. Dipping the base in hormone rooting powder will increase your chances of success but is not strictly necessary.

Insert cuttings, using a dibber, into a pot or tray of cutting compost to just below the lowest leaf (2), making sure that they are firm and evenly spaced. Cover the pot either with a plastic dome or contruct a tent using a polythene bag and bent wire or short sticks (3). Place in a warm, shady position, but not in direct sunlight to limit the amount of water loss. Give the cuttings gradually more exposure as they develop. Water regularly, keeping the soil moist but not wet. They can be potted on or planted out as soon as roots have developed.

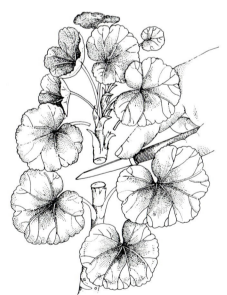

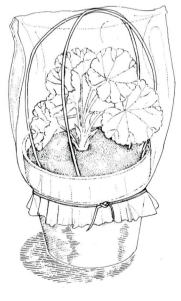

SOFTWOOD CUTTINGS

1. Select a healthy shoot, and take a cutting just below a leaf joint. Remove leaves from the bottom third of the cutting.

2. Use a dibber to insert the cutting in a pot of cutting compost, with the bottom third of the cutting covered.

3. Cover the pot with a polythene bag supported by a frame of bent wires, and tied at the opening with a piece of string.

SEMI-HARD CUTTINGS These can be taken, usually in midsummer, from plants such as heathers, rosemary or fuchsia that form a semi-woody stem and from many conifers. Cut a shoot 6–8in (15–20cm) in length, either from the main stem or from a side shoot. Remove the lower leaves and cut off the soft tip, which will otherwise wilt. Then follow the softwood planting technique. Rooting should take 2–3 weeks and the cuttings must then be hardened off as for softwood. Protect the cuttings from frost over the winter; ideally in a cold frame, and the young plants will be ready to plant out late the following spring, discarding any cuttings that have not rooted.

SEMI-HARD CUTTINGS
Cut a side-shoot approximately 6in (15cm) long from a semi-hardwood such as rosemary (1). Using a sharp knife, remove the lower leaves and the soft tip from your cutting (2).

1

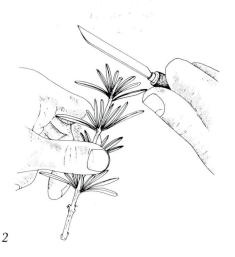

2

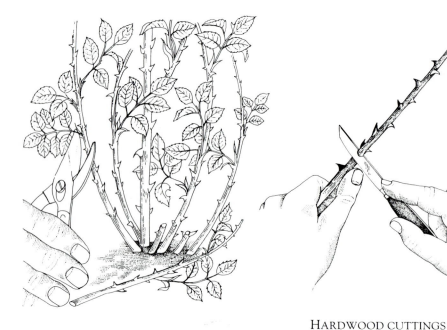

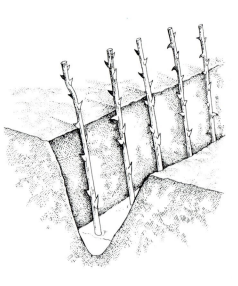

HARDWOOD CUTTINGS

1. Cut stems approximately 6in (15cm) from the base of the plant.

2. Trim the cutting to an approximate length of 12in (30cm).

3. Plant outdoors in a sand-lined trench approximately 8in (20cm) deep.

HARDWOOD CUTTINGS Select stems that are woody but, ideally, not yet very hard. The cuttings are usually taken from the end of summer to the middle of autumn. Cut the stems near the base (1) and trim to approximately 12in (30cm). If the stem is long you can use one stem to produce two or more cuttings (2). Make the cuts just below a bud or joint at the base and just above a bud at the top of the cutting. Plant outdoors in a sheltered spot in a sand-lined narrow trench. Approximately two-thirds of the cutting should be below ground level (3). Push soil back into the trench and tread in firmly.

You need do nothing to these cuttings apart from watering when the weather is dry and removing weeds. Leave in position for a year to eighteen months to allow roots to develop, then carefully move your new plants to their permanent positions, or into a nursery bed.

'IRISHMAN'S CUTTINGS' These are not strictly cuttings but a form of division. It is used for plants such as violas, hardy fuchsias, early-flowering chrysanthemums, campanulas and other herbaceous material. This is also a successful method of propagating house plants such as sensevieria (mother-in-law's tongue). Ease off single stems with sufficiently large root systems to be independent, and plant out in spring to early autumn.

TAKING IRISHMAN'S CUTTINGS
Gently loosen the soil around the plant with a garden fork to prevent damaging the roots. Ease off single stems, taking care that their root systems are large enough to support them independently.

DIVISION

Division is the simplest method of propagation for plants with a clump of ground-level shoots. Herbaceous perennials with fibrous, densely matted crowns, such as monarda and heleniums, can be increased easily in spring and autumn by digging and dividing. To make division easier, shorten the stems and shake off as much soil as possible (1). Break off sections with your fingers, or cut woody crowns with a knife. Large, solid clumps can be divided by pushing two forks back to back into the centre of the clump and forcing them apart (2). Divide further, in the same way, until you are left with pieces consisting of about six stems, making sure each has roots and bud growth. Cut away any woody stems and dead shoots, and replant.

DIVISION
Divide an established plant by loosening the surrounding soil and freeing the roots. Insert two garden forks back to back in the middle of the plant, and lever the clump apart. Division not only increases your stock of plants, it also helps to perpetuate established stock which might otherwise deteriorate through overcrowding.

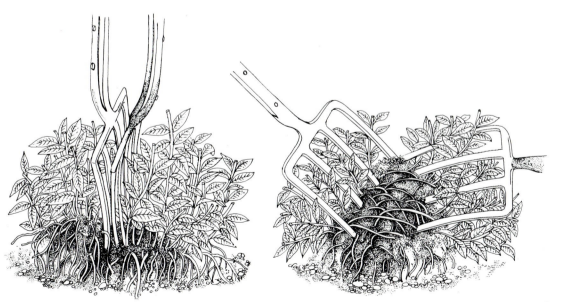

PRUNING

To reap the greatest reward from your shrubs, it is essential to learn at least the basic principles of pruning. Do not be put off by what appears at first glance to be a highly technical procedure – much of it is common sense, once you understand the growing and flowering habits of your shrubs. Evergreen trees and shrubs require little pruning – only removal of old, overgrown, damaged or diseased stems.

MAKING THE CUTS Stems that are left ragged may die back and damage a new bud. Use secateurs, a pruning saw, and lopping shears for cutting high branches. Keep all your equipment well sharpened. Cut just above an outward facing bud or pair of buds at a gentle angle away from the bud – not so close that the bud could be damaged and not so far up the stem that the stem could die back. Dispose of all the prunings carefully and mulch around the base of a shrub after hard pruning.

DECIDUOUS TREES AND SHRUBS Pruning is determined by the season the shrub flowers and whether it flowers on wood made the previous season or the current one. Those that produce flowers on new wood tend to do so later in the year; those that flower on old wood, flower earlier, before the new wood develops. Make certain before pruning that the shrub actually needs it.

NEW WOOD Shrubs that flower on new wood, usually after midsummer such as *Buddleia davidii*, hardy fuchsias, autumn flowering clematis and Hybrid Tea roses, can be cut hard back in the spring before the new growth starts. Cut back all the previous year's growth to 2–3 buds from their base. Cutting back into the older wood may harm the plant. Remove entirely any weak, damaged or straggling shoots.

OLD WOOD Shrubs that flower in the early summer – forsythia, philadelphus, weigela and deutzia, for example – can be pruned immediately after flowering. Remove all dead, damaged and weak growth completely, then cut back the stems that have borne flowers to within two or three buds of the junction with the main stem where new young shoots are growing, to encourage new growth. In addition cut back, almost to ground level, wood that is more than five years old and becoming less productive.

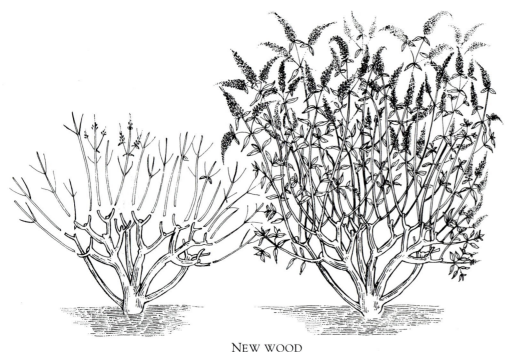

NEW WOOD
Cut back in spring to encourage new wood which will produce a wealth of flowers in mid to late summer.

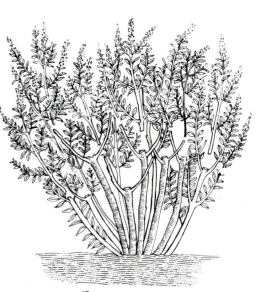

OLD WOOD
Prune shrubs that flower in early summer immediately after flowering.

ROSES Species and old shrub roses require little pruning, just general maintenance and shaping.

Prune Hybrid Teas hard in early spring to an outward facing bud leaving only 8–12in (20–30cm) of growth. Floribundas need less heavy pruning, but you should tidy your bushes and remove all weak wood.

CLIMBERS The early treatment of climbers is important. You will want them to have a good framework and to achieve this you should have trellis work or a tidy system of vine eyes and wire all ready to support your plants. Thereafter, pruning is mostly common sense based on whether your plant flowers on new or old wood and whether you wish it to be formally trained against the wall or given more freedom and an exuberant natural style.

CLEMATIS There are three main groups of clematis, each of which requires slightly different treatment. Two useful tips: attach the label with the name to the support not to the stem of the clematis which you may prune away, and write on the back of the label 'none', 'hard' or 'light'.

NONE These include the early flowering clematis such as the Alpinas, Macropetalas, Montanas and C. *armandii*. They need no pruning.

HARD These include the late-flowering varieties which flower on the current year's growth, such as the Jackmanii group, Viticellas, C. *texensis*, C. *orientalis* and C. *tangutica*. Prune these in late winter to strong buds 1–3ft (30–90cm) from the ground. Pruned lightly they will flower too high to be appreciated.

LIGHT These include the early summer-flowering, large-flowered Patens group such as 'Nelly Moser', 'Lasurstern', 'The President' and 'Marie Boisselot'. They flower both on new growth and on the stems made the previous year. Remove weak growth and some of the old wood in late winter, leaving enough for an early summer flowering on the old wood. They should have a second flush of flowers on their new growth in mid to late summer.

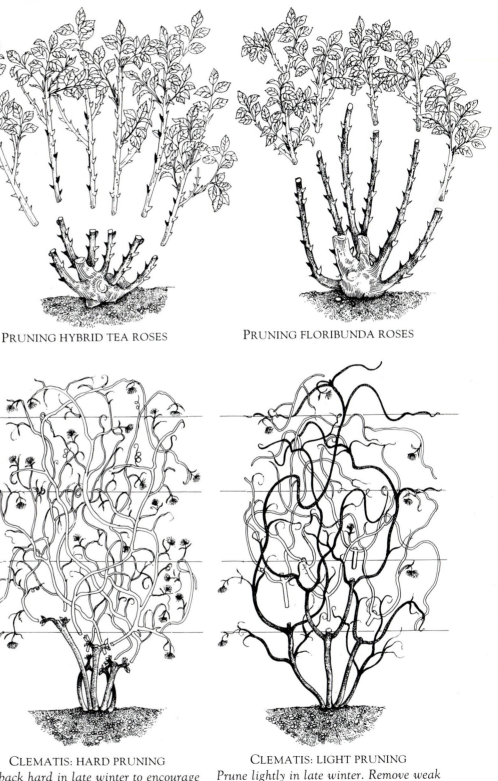

PRUNING HYBRID TEA ROSES

PRUNING FLORIBUNDA ROSES

CLEMATIS: HARD PRUNING
Cut back hard in late winter to encourage ample flowers the following summer and autumn.

CLEMATIS: LIGHT PRUNING
Prune lightly in late winter. Remove weak growth and some old wood, leaving enough old wood for early-summer flowering.

BORDER UPKEEP

Try to keep on top of the jobs that must be carried out in the garden during the year. If you deal with the small tasks as they present themselves it will take much less time than if you leave something to become a problem.

Remove weeds when they are small and have not had a chance to form deep root systems and certainly before they seed. Keep a close eye out for any signs of pests or disease and act immediately. Protect by spraying early with fungicides and pesticides. During dry spells, water before the soil dries out completely – in spring if necessary – and carry on watering until autumn. Give plants a good soak: it is absolutely pointless merely to sprinkle the surface with water which will only encourage roots to come to the surface searching for water.

Herbaceous plants, such as monarda, will become thin in the centre of the clump after several seasons' growth and require renovation. Lift and divide the clump, in autumn, or in spring if your soil is very heavy. Discard the centre. Replant the new plants at the same depth as the original plants. Not all plants respond well to this treatment, however, so check first.

Carry out general cutting back and tidying up straggling branches or stems at any time during the year, but particularly in autumn and winter. Do not immediately relegate the stems to the compost heap or bonfire – perhaps they could be used in a flower arrangement. Take them indoors and dry them, and they will keep looking good for several months when there is little other material around.

MULCHING

Mulching is probably one of the most underestimated, least widely practised but most worthwhile tasks to be carried out in the garden. It involves applying a layer of organic matter around the base of shrubs and hardy perennials in spring. A mulch insulates the soil during cold spells in spring, keeps it cool in hot weather, and reduces moisture loss in dry periods. It also reduces the number of weeds. A mulch can be leaf mould, well-rotted farmyard manure, mushroom compost, peat, pulverized bark or even the contents of used growing bags. Some types of organic matter, such as peat and bark, will add no nutrients to the soil, but will act as excellent soil conditioners. You should apply a mulch

in conjunction with a fertilizer according to your soil requirements.

Apply the mulch to the soil when it is moist but not waterlogged. Prepare the soil by removing all weeds and rotting vegetation, and water well if the soil is dry. Apply a spring feed if you have not already done so.

Lay a 2–3in (5–7.5cm) layer of mulch around the base of the plants, but do not apply it right up to the stem which could cause it to rot. In the autumn any mulch remaining should be forked into the soil. This will help to improve both the texture and the quality of the soil.

FERTILIZING

Organic or inorganic fertilizers will give the soil a boost at the beginning of the growing season to promote healthy and productive growth. No two fertilizers will produce the same results and it is important to choose an all-purpose fertilizer or one which specifically suits the needs of your soil and your crop. The aim is to replace the vital nutrients that are either lacking in your soil or that are constantly washed away by watering and rain.

Nitrogen, phosphorus and potassium are the main nutrients, while others

MULCHING

A mulch will vastly improve the condition of a shrub (right) or herbaceous plant (far right). In spring, fork a layer of organic matter around the base of the plant, taking care to keep the mulch from contact with the plant stem, which might cause the latter to rot.

such as calcium, magnesium and sulphur are present in much smaller quantities. Nitrogen promotes rapid growth and lush green leaves; when it is required plants turn yellow and lack vigour. Phosphorus is for general fertility but particularly encourages strong root development and healthy seedlings. Potassium encourages high productivity and an intense colour in flowers and fruit, as well as improving the general resistance of the plants to pests and diseases. For general spring fertilizing you should buy a good all-purpose fertilizer, such as Growmore, which contains the three vital nutrients, nitrogen, phosphorus and potassium in equal proportions. It is easy to use and will suit most of your needs. Check, however, that the plants actually need to be fed; they may be quite happy growing under infertile conditions.

A slow-release organic fertilizer such as bonemeal, applied in spring, is a useful and readily available source of phosphorus, which is excellent for herbaceous perennials. In summer apply a liquid fertilizer, which will release nutrients rapidly – choose one that is higher in potassium for vigorous growth and good colour.

STAKING

Tall herbaceous plants, which at full height tend to droop or bend under the weight of their flowers, need extra support. Stake the surrounding soil in spring while the plants are still small and the growth not too advanced. Do not leave staking until after the plant has collapsed – the damage will have been done. Do not tie too tightly or the plant's growth may be restricted. There are various methods that can be used.

Wire frames or canes are the sturdiest, most popular supports for plants that grow to more than 5ft (1.5m). A simple and cheaper alternative for slightly shorter plants is just to use bamboo canes and garden twine. This type of staking is suitable for plants between 2–4ft (60–120cm) in height. Pea sticks are suitable for lower bushy herbaceous plants up to 2ft (60cm) high, that may have floppy heads.

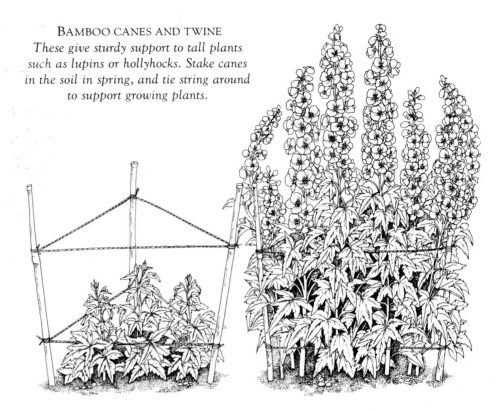

BAMBOO CANES AND TWINE
These give sturdy support to tall plants such as lupins or hollyhocks. Stake canes in the soil in spring, and tie string around to support growing plants.

PEA STICKS
Pea sticks will support low-growing herbaceous plants, the weight of whose flower heads might otherwise cause the plant stem to droop or even break.

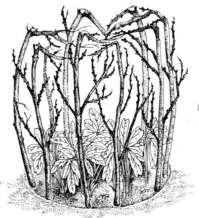

ARRANGING FRESH FLOWERS

Bringing fresh flowers into your home is one of life's greatest pleasures. But to transfer flowers successfully indoors from their natural environment requires a combination of instinct, practice and a little acquired technical skill.

CUTTING FLOWERS

The ideal time to pick flowers is early in the morning before the sun strips them of valuable water content, or in the early evening when they have been well fed and nourished. Put flowers cut during the day in water straight away and leave to soak in a cool place for several hours.

Pick flowers such as peonies, irises, tulips, lilies and gladioli when they are in loose bud with some colour showing; the buds should then develop naturally in the vase. However, do not cut roses in tight bud as they may not open in water. Do not pick flowers at the height of their beauty, as they will last no longer than a day or two in an arrangement. Those flowers that have already developed pollen or whose buds are fully open are in the last stages of their cycle and will start dropping their petals very soon. Avoid blooms with weak stems, or discoloured leaves or petals.

Spring-flowering bulbs should be cut well into the green part of the stem; the lower white section does not take up water well in an arrangement.

Secateurs and a sharp knife are all you need take for cutting, but ideally you should also carry a bucket half-filled with water to put the stems in as you cut them; otherwise soak the flowers in water immediately you get indoors.

CONDITIONING

When the stem of a flower is cut, the cells which take up the water are crushed and the vital water supply cut off. A newly cut stem begins to scale over immediately and an airlock may form. Water is crucial to the well-being of the flower, and conditioning makes it possible for the plant to take it up.

There are various methods of conditioning depending on the nature of the stem, but in all cases the stems must be recut. With a sharp knife make cuts approximately 2in (5cm) up the stem. It is best to make the cut on a diagonal slant with the stems plunged in water; in this way free water intake is assured. Remove leaves below water level; they will rot and encourage bacteria to form. This is particularly important for dahlias, lilac and philadelphus whose leaves also take a lot of water from the stem, depriving the flowers.

Put the stems in fresh, cold, but not icy, water up to their necks. Leave them in a cool place for several hours to take in water. Young green stems do not need to be soaked for as long as older woody stems; a young stem can become waterlogged – two hours' soaking is usually enough. Do not soak grey foliage, it will lose its greyness.

Certain stems require specific conditioning treatments.

CONDITIONING FLOWERS
Soak flowers up to their necks in cold water for a few hours
Tightly wrap bent stems in damp newspaper to straighten them.

WOODY STEMS Scrape off the bark to about 2in (5cm) up the stem and remove any thorns. Split the scraped ends vertically and plunge the stem ends in boiling water for 30 seconds. Protect the heads from rising steam by wrapping them in plastic bags or newspapers. Put them immediately into cool water up to their necks. Flowers which require this type of treatment include camellias, rhododendrons, lilac, chrysanthemums, hydrangeas and roses.

HOLLOW STEMS Recut straight across rather than at an angle. Hold the stems upside down and, using a houseplant watering can, fill the stem with water. Stopper this end with a dampened plug of cotton wool. This treatment will prolong the life of flowers such as lupins, amaryllis and delphiniums.

BLEEDING STEMS Some stems 'bleed' a milky sap which blocks the intake of water. To prevent the fluid from coagulating, singe the cut ends over a flame for several seconds to seal the pores from which the sap comes, and place directly into cool water. This treatment is used for such plants as poppies, euphorbias and zinnias. Spring bulb flowers should be soaked overnight to drain off the sap which causes the water to foul.

FOLIAGE Remove excess leaves on the lower part of the stem, split the stem ends – or crush them if they are very large and tough – and immerse in water for several hours.

TRANSPORTING CUT FLOWERS

Flowers quickly wilt in the back of a car on a warm day. Condition them thoroughly before transporting, and then either lay them in a florist's box surrounded by damp paper, or wedge a half-filled bucket of water behind the front seat. In cold weather insulate with layers of newspaper; flowers are just as susceptible to cold as to heat. If you have to pick flowers well in advance of arranging, keep them in a cool dark place, which will slow down their development. Alternatively, flowers can be kept fresh by putting the stem ends in a plastic bag lined with wet paper or moss and sealing the bag.

THE MECHANICS OF FLOWER ARRANGING

Achieving a beautiful arrangement of flowers does not require a vast outlay on tools and gadgets, but some basic equipment does make more adventurous arrangements possible.

PLASTIC FOAM Blocks and pre-cut shapes of plastic foam, used for supporting flower stems at practically any angle, are available from most florists. Cut large blocks with a sharp knife to fit your container – the foam should sit just above the rim.

Cover the dry foam with water and leave it to soak until bubbles have stopped rising to the surface, usually about 15 minutes but this varies with different brands. Once fully soaked the foam should not be allowed to dry out. The structure of the foam alters and it becomes crumbly and unreliable when resoaked. Place it in a sealed plastic bag until ready to use.

Push the stems about 1in (2.5cm) into the foam. Use an awl or equivalent to make holes in the plastic foam for soft or delicate stems. For medium to large arrangements, wrap chicken wire around the foam and secure it in position to give more support.

CHICKEN WIRE This is especially good for supporting arrangements with spring flowers and heavier stems and branches. Use it in vases with fairly wide

necks. Buy chicken wire with a 2in (5cm) mesh; this is the most suitable for general arrangements. It can either be used scrunched up in the bottom of a container and secured to the edges with florist's wire or string, or simply hooked across the top of a container and secured with adhesive florist's tape or electrician's tape. It can also be used in conjunction with plastic foam or a pinholder. The only drawbacks are that the wire tends to scratch the side of a container, will rust if left in water for too long, and can look unsightly in a transparent container. It should always be washed and dried thoroughly after use. Alternatively, use green plastic-coated chicken wire.

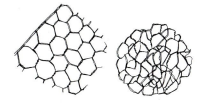

PINHOLDERS Metal pinholders are inset with regularly spaced nails on which to impale stems. They are relatively expensive, but if you buy one with a base about 3in (7.5cm) in diameter it will suit most of your needs and should last indefinitely. The plastic variety will not support heavier arrangements. Pinholders come in various densities, either packed tight with nails for use with more delicate, fine-stemmed flowers or with more widely spaced nails for larger woody stems.

For extra stability, attach pieces of plasticine or florist's clay to the base of the pinholder and press it firmly into the container. Pinholders are particularly useful for displaying sprays of blossom in shallow containers.

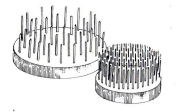

SECATEURS AND FLORIST'S SCISSORS When cutting flowers and foliage for arranging, use secateurs and florist's scissors with serrated edges rather than ordinary scissors which crush and damage the stems. Florist's scissors with a wire-cutting notch can also be used for removing thorns and stripping bark.

PLASTICINE, FLORIST'S CLAY, STRING, WIRE AND TAPE These can all be used for securing and stabilizing the mechanics of an arrangement. All surfaces must be completely dry when using plasticine or clay, or it will not stick firmly.

MISTER AND WATERING CAN A fine spray of mist once a day should maintain the moisture levels of plastic foam and flowers. Aim just above the arrangement and the mist will settle naturally on the flowers and foliage. A watering can with a long fine spout can be used for topping up water levels in vases without disturbing the arrangement.

FLORIST'S VIAL These are clear plastic or metal containers used for holding single stems. A vial will extend the life of an individual flower in a mixed display of fruit or dried flowers, and they can also be used to incorporate short-stemmed flowers in a bouquet of predominantly long-stemmed flowers.

PEBBLES, SAND AND GRAVEL   Natural materials can be used to add visual interest and contrast to plant material and act as ballast for a top-heavy arrangement to prevent it from toppling over. They can also be used to disguise unattractive mechanics – particularly in a transparent container.

MOSS This can be bought from a florist or picked in your garden. It must be soaked before use and stored wet in a sealed plastic bag. It is useful for disguising the mechanics of an arrangement. There are a number of varieties frequently used in flower arrangements. Bun moss is the velvety-green variety often to be found in the garden. Sphagnum moss holds water like a sponge. The silvery-grey variety of lichen is useful for winter arrangements. It is brittle when dry and often used in dried-flower arrangements, but becomes rubbery and manageable when soaked.

CONTAINERS

If an arrangement is to succeed it must be in harmony with its container, but almost anything can be brought into use from an egg cup to a crystal family heirloom – each has its place.

A few basic shapes will stand you in good stead. Have a tall, narrow vase for displaying single stems, one or two shallow containers for arrangements across a table and a couple of tall, large

STEMS SUPPORTED BY MARBLES
IN A GLASS VASE

vases for displaying bulkier combinations. Choose one that will take heavy stems and branches of blossom in the spring and large dried arrangements.

China and pottery vases are invaluable, requiring no special preparation; but a careful eye is needed with highly patterned vases.

Glass containers must be kept scrupulously clean; changing the water frequently will prevent bacteria building up. Remove all foliage below the water level. Use pebbles or even marbles in a glass container to support stems.

Make sure metal containers are completely watertight and remove any stubborn stains with lemon juice and salt, or vinegar and salt. Rinse all metal thoroughly before use. Ideally, use plastic-coated chicken wire or plastic foam to support an arrangement to prevent scratching the metal.

Wood and basketware may need to be made watertight with a lining of silver foil or dampened foam, or containers specifically sold for this purpose, or just household plastic containers.

CREATING AN ARRANGEMENT

Before starting to arrange your flowers, think about the mood you want to create, the flowers and containers you have available, and where the arrangement is going to stand. Although there are formulae for creating different shapes of formal arrangement, these are less fashionable now and there are no hard-and-fast rules.

SCALE A sense of proportion, both in the arrangement itself and in relation to its position and the way it will be viewed, is the key to a successful arrangement. Clearly, if it is to be a focal point, viewed from a distance, it needs to be fairly large and dramatic. Fine variations of colour will be lost. A little posy to be viewed from close to can, if you wish, be much more subtle.

Consider the height of the container and the angle from which you are going to be looking at the arrangement. If the vase is tall and to be seen from the side, the flowers should be in proportion to

POSIES GROUPED IN JUGS OF
VARYING SIZES

the vase – one and a half times the height is a good guideline – otherwise the arrangement will look squat. If the vase is standing at floor level and looked at from on top, the flowers can be shorter in relation to it. The same applies to a wider vase or bowl. If it is to be viewed from the side the arrangement must be taller than it would be if it is viewed from above.

However you arrange your flowers, stand back and view the arrangement at frequent intervals from the angle at which you will view it in its final position – instinct will quickly tell you whether the proportions are working.

If you feel uncertain to begin with about creating a very large arrangement, you can create an equally dramatic effect by grouping a collection of smaller posies in vases.

FOLLOWING NATURAL LINES Consider the way the flowers you have in front of you were growing in the garden. Aim to take advantage of their natural shape and inclination, rather than forcing them into awkward positions.

Use flowers that are naturally upright at the back of an arrangement to give height; delphiniums, lupins, hollyhocks, irises, acanthus – all these are stately flowers that need to hold their heads high to be seen at their best.

Flowers with heavy, impressive heads

such as roses and peonies should be placed at the centre of a large arrangement; they will naturally draw the eye in. Placed on the periphery they will cause imbalance in the arrangement both literally and visually.

Stems that naturally trail or curve – ivy and small clematis, for example, or sprays of tiny roses – are perfect for draping over the vase and filling the base of an arrangement.

Give your arrangement depth by using flower stems of different lengths. If all the heads are on the same plane the arrangement will seem two-dimensional. Take advantage of natural differences in flower height.

BUNCHING IN THE HAND A natural, free-flowing arrangement is perhaps the easiest to achieve. This is often most effective if the flowers are gathered together in your hand before being placed in the vase. The same technique can be used when putting together posies to give as presents.

To achieve a natural look you need to spiral the stems, adding each stem at a slight angle and turning the bunch as you build it up. Stagger the length of the stems from the centre. When the bunch is complete, trim the ends and then tie it with raffia or string, or place it in a vase with a relatively narrow neck by squeezing the stems together. The arrangement will then fall open naturally. If you do not spiral the stems they will stay stiff and upright. The technique takes a little practice, but it will soon become easy.

AFTERCARE

Try to position your arrangement in as cool a place as possible, away from draughts and sources of heat. Wilting flowers can often be simply revived by repeating the conditioning processes. Top up the vase once a day. Spraying will replace water loss caused by central heating. Snip out dead flower heads.

There are many recipes for cut flower nutrient and several proprietary brands, but the best formula is fresh water changed every day. Heavy-handedness with a nutrient can foul the water.

CREATING A LARGE ARRANGEMENT
The natural lines of flowers as they grow in the garden inspire this arrangement: tall delphiniums back heavy-headed roses, with trailers at the front.

BUNCHING IN THE HAND
Spiral the stems, turning the bunch as you build it up with flowers.

An arrangement bunched in the hand will fall open naturally in the vase.

DRYING FLOWERS

Almost every flower and leaf can be preserved in some way, and drying flowers at home means that when the freshness and beauty of your garden have faded the flowers and foliage will still be delicately preserved.

Pick flowers for drying on a dry day. If slightly wet or dewy they will take longer to dehydrate, and the quicker they dry, the better the colour. The flowers should be as near perfect as possible. Cut them just before they reach their peak. Gather leaves in late summer before they begin to change colour.

There are three basic methods of drying: air drying, desiccants and glycerine. They all require very little basic equipment, but plenty of space for drying and some patience.

AIR DRYING

Choose a well-ventilated, cool, dry, dark room – an attic, spare bedroom or dry garage would all be suitable spots.

Direct sunlight causes the drying flowers to discolour and damp causes mildew. Flowers can either be hung upside down, or dried upright or flat. HANGING Flowers can be successfully dried in large quantities by this method. Remove all the lower leaves and wipe away any moisture. Tie the stems into bunches adjusting the flowers so that the heads touch as little as possible.

Hang the bunches from a rail or string suspended across the drying area. Make sure that the bunches do not touch each other. Check regularly. Air drying can take from three weeks to three months. The stems must be completely dry before you take them down. They should feel crisp to the touch. Flowers that have not been properly dried will disintegrate rapidly.

This method is suitable for: acanthus, *Alchemilla mollis*, *Achillea filipendulina*, *Amaranthus caudatus*, astilbe, astrantia, calendula, dahlia, delphinium, *Gypso-*

phila paniculata, helichrysum, hydrangea, lavender, lunaria, statice, *Stachys lanata*, *Nigella damascena*, peony, *Physalis alkekengi*, ranunculus, salvia, xeranthemum.

DRYING UPRIGHT Hydrangeas and many of the seed heads and grasses are most successfully dried upright. Pick the material for drying when it is almost dry on the plant for best results. Put $\frac{1}{2}$in (1cm) of water in a container tall enough to support the stems. Place the stems in the container and leave until the water has evaporated or the stems feel totally dry.

This method is suitable for: *Achillea filipendulina*, *Amaranthus caudatus*, *Gypsophila paniculata*, hydrangea, lunaria, rose, santolina.

DRYING FLAT Many leaves, particularly deciduous ones, will dry well laid flat in a box or on a clean, dry floor. Larger heads such as artichokes, thistles, proteas or maize can be dried this way supported by chicken wire.

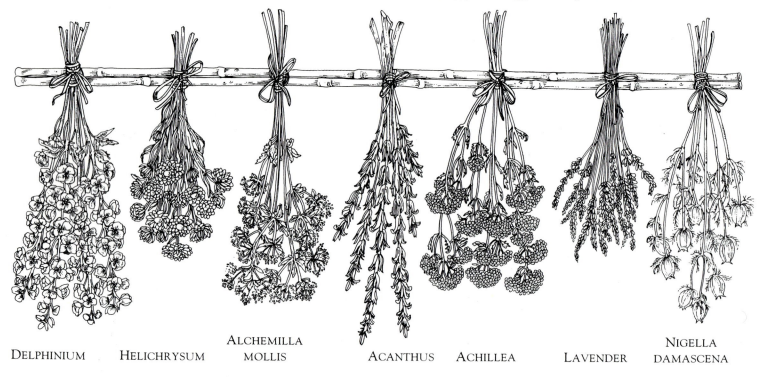

DELPHINIUM   HELICHRYSUM   ALCHEMILLA MOLLIS   ACANTHUS   ACHILLEA   LAVENDER   NIGELLA DAMASCENA

DESICCANTS

These dry out the moisture from the petals and calyx leaving the colour and shape almost perfectly preserved – even retaining, in some cases, the scent.

SILICA GEL Chemists and shops selling flower-arranging equipment are usually the best sources of silica gel. It is the most expensive desiccant, but can be re-used almost indefinitely. It comes in different grades – either coarse crystals or fine, white sugar-like grains. The crystals are sometimes dyed with a blue/pink moisture indicator – blue when completely dry and pink when moisture has been absorbed. This helps to gauge when flowers have dried through, but with a little practice you will be able to tell simply by gently touching the petals. The finer gel gives the best results, but the coarse crystals can be ground down in a food-processor or coffee grinder. Clean it out thoroughly after use.

To dry out the gel for re-use, place it on a baking tray in a warm oven and leave for 1–2 hours. Switch off the oven and open the door slightly and leave to cool. Use the gel immediately to ensure that it is used completely dry.

BORAX AND ALUM Fine silver sand is usually mixed with these desiccants, 2 parts sand to 1 part borax or alum. Very delicate or fleshy stems may be damaged under the weight of the sand and fleshy flowers sometimes go mouldy in borax.

SILICA GEL
Covering flower heads with silica gel.

USING DESICCANTS Put a 1in (2.5cm) layer of desiccant in an air-tight tin or plastic container. Lay the flower heads gently on top, face upwards, making sure that they do not touch, and pile the desiccant gently around them. Use a fine brush to work the desiccant in between the petals making sure every part is totally covered.

The best results are obtained if the stem is removed and the head is wired, but if you want to retain the natural stems, make small holes in the base of the container and push the stems through so that the flower head sits on a layer of the desiccant. Place the container on an upright cardboard box to allow the stems to hang freely and to catch any falling desiccant.

Check flowers dried in silica gel after 48 hours, but other desiccants may take from ten days to three weeks. Flowers left for too long will become brittle.

This method is suitable for: alstroemeria, amaryllis, calendula, camellia, clematis, dahlia, dianthus, freesia, helleborus, lillium, narcissus, peony, *Polygonatum × hybridum*, primula, ranunculus, rose, rudbeckia, scabious, tulip, viola, zinnia.

GLYCERINE

Flowers and leaves are not dried out by this method; instead the water content is replaced by glycerine. This leaves the plant material strong and pliable. It is most successful with foliage. Pick branches of mature deciduous leaves in late summer before they begin to change colour. Pick evergreen leaves at any time of the year.

Crush woody stems and strip the bark. Prune out any leaves that are damaged or overcrowding.

Make up a preserving solution consisting of 1 part glycerine to 2 parts very hot water. Stir well. Add a quarter of a teaspoon of chlorohexidine to prevent bacterial growth. Fill a tall container with 2in (5cm) of the solution and rest the stem or stems in it.

Place in a cool dark place. Check regularly and do not allow the glycerine solution to dry out – replenish as necessary. Leave to soak for one to ten weeks

GLYCERINE
Preserving flower stems with glycerine.

depending on the leaf type. The process is complete when all the leaves have turned colour and before beads of glycerine have begun to appear on them. Remove the stems from the solution, wash and rinse thoroughly and pat dry with a tea-cloth or kitchen paper.

Single leaves can be preserved by immersing them in a slightly stronger solution. Wash and rinse after preserving and pat dry. Wire if necessary.

Do not store leaves preserved with glycerine with plants that have been dried, the moisture in the glycerine will cause them to rot.

This method is suitable for: beech, choisya, eucalyptus, holly, hosta, hydrangea, ivy, mahonia, *Molucella laevis*, *Polygonatum × hybridum*.

WIRING FLOWERS FOR DRYING

If a flower stem is too fragile, too thick or too short you may need to wire it. Wiring can be carried out either before or after drying – with delicate flowers it may be best to do it beforehand.

Choose a wire that will look natural, is heavy enough to support the flower head and is fairly pliable. Wrap the wire stem with florist's binding tape. If the flower head is heavy, wire cane to the stem. Flowers with a firm, flat centre, such as helichrysum, can be wired by bending the end of a piece of stiff wire and threading it through the centre of the flower until the loop has caught.

INDEX

ACKNOWLEDGMENTS

The publisher thanks the following photographers and organizations for their kind permission to reproduce the photographs in this book:

2 Linda Burgess/Insight; 10–11 Jerry Harpur (The Priory, Kemerton); 14 above Photos Horticultural; 14 below Harry Smith Collection; 15 Lamontagne; 18 Jerry Harpur (Jenkyn Place, Bentley, Somerset); 19 Tania Midgley; 20 above Tania Midgley; 20 below George Wright/Octopus; 21 Jerry Harpur (Tintinhull House, Somerset); 22 Tania Midgley; 23–26 Lamontagne; 27 Andrew Lawson; 28 Jacqui Hurst; 29 Lamontagne; 30 Philippe Perdereau; 31 left Tania Midgley; 31 right Hugh Palmer (Harlow Car Gardens); 36 Garden Picture Library/Ron Sutherland; 37 Lamontagne; 42–43 Philippe Perdereau; 44 Marijke Heuff; 45 Philippe Perdereau; 46 Jacqui Hurst; 47 above Philippe Perdereau; 47 centre Jerry Harpur (designer Ken Akers, Great Saling); 47 below Eric Crichton; 53 Lamontagne; 80 above Linda Burgess/Insight; 81 Linda Burgess/Insight; 88–89 La Maison de Marie Claire (Hussenot/Puech); 100–101 Garden Picture Library/Ron Sutherland; 102 above Eric Crichton; 102 below Photos Horticultural; 103 left Derek Gould; 103 centre and right Photos Horticultural; 104 left Photos Horticultural; 104 centre Eric Crichton; 104 right Lamontagne; 105 left Lamontagne; 105 centre Harry Smith Collection; 105 right Photos Horticultural; 106 left MAP/Annette Schreiner; 106 centre and right Eric Crichton; 107 left Photos Horticultural; 107 centre Eric Crichton; 107 right Photos Horticultural; 108 left Andrew Lawson; 108 centre MAP/Annette Schreiner; 108 right Lamontagne; 109 left and centre Eric Crichton; 109 right Lamontagne; 110 left and centre Eric Crichton; 110 right Lamontagne; 111 left Lamontagne; 111 centre Photos Horticultural; 111 right MAP/Annette Schreiner; 112 left Derek Gould; 112 centre and right Tania Midgley; 113 left and above right Photos Horticultural; 113 centre right Tania Midgley; 113 below right Eric Crichton; 114 left Eric Crichton; 114 centre Andrew Lawson; 114 right Photos Horticultural; 115 left Photos Horticultural; 115 centre Eric Crichton; 115 right Photos Horticultural; 116 left and centre Lamontagne; 116 right Photos Horticultural; 117 left Photos Horticultural; 117 centre Eric Crichton; 117 right Lamontagne; 118 left and centre Eric Crichton; 118 right Andrew Lawson; 119 left Eric Crichton; 119 centre Tania Midgley; 119 right MAP/Annette Schreiner; 120 left Eric Crichton; 120 centre and right Lamontagne; 121 left Photos Horticultural; 121 centre Karl Dietrich Buhler/Elizabeth Whiting & Associates; 121 right Photos Horticultural; 122 left Tania Midgley; 122 centre Andrew Lawson; 122 right Lamontagne; 123 left and right Andrew Lawson; 123 centre Photos Horticultural.

Special photography – Linda Burgess 1, 6–7, 8, 13, 56–75, 76–79, 80 below, 82–83, 85–87, 92–99, 124–5; Jacqui Hurst 76 left, 84, 90–91.

FLOWER ARRANGEMENTS

All flower arrangements were created by Linda Burgess except for those listed below.
Jacket front and back Fiona Barnett; 60 bottom Rosemary Verey; 62 Rosemary Verey; 64 bottom Fiona Barnett; 72–75 Fiona Barnett; 76 Ernestine Dyer; 77 Fiona Barnett; 82–84 Fiona Barnett; 88–89 La Maison de Marie Claire; 90 top Jacqui Hurst; 90 bottom Ernestine Dyer; 91 Jacqui Hurst; 92–93 Fiona Barnett; 96–97 Fiona Barnett; 98 Ernestine Dyer; 99 top and bottom left Ernestine Dyer; 99 bottom centre Rosemary Verey.